D0960165

Mastering Ministry's Pressure Points

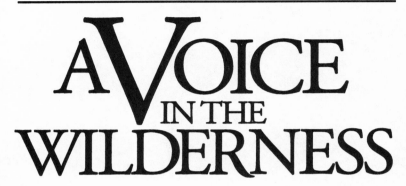

A VOICE IN THE WILDERNESS

Clear Preaching in a Complicated World

STEVE BROWN
HADDON ROBINSON
WILLIAM WILLIMON

MULTNOMAH BOOKS

A VOICE IN THE WILDERNESS
© 1993 by Christianity Today, Inc.

Published by Multnomah Press Books
Questar Publishers, Inc.
Sisters, Oregon

Printed in the United States of America

International Standard Book Number: 0-88070-589-2

93 94 95 96 97 98 99 00 01 — 10 9 8 7 6 5 4 3 2 1

Contents

Introduction

Even the great preachers have spent time in the preaching wilderness, talking to arid landscapes of cactus-like people. Take Martin Luther, clearly one of the best preachers Christendom has produced.

Luther had been preaching in his Wittenberg church for years, but the longer he preached, the more discouraged he grew. People just didn't get it. They gladly heard him, but instead of being inspired to discipleship, they only became lethargic. Luther noted that despite his preaching, "no one acts accordingly, but instead the people become so crude, cold, and lazy that it is a shame, and they do much less than before."

For instance, when Luther and the reformers started teaching that attending worship was no longer a meritorious act, that it earned people nothing in God's eyes, people applauded. They no doubt thought it a relief to hear that worship was first a gracious opportunity to thank God and hear his Word in freedom. Nonetheless, worship attendance dropped.

In January 1530, Luther was so fed up, he announced to the congregation that he refused to preach any longer — essentially he went on strike. Of course, Luther couldn't stay away from the pulpit for long.

Still, discouragement dogged him his entire life. A year before he died, while on a trip, he determined not to return to Wittenberg, his home town, the center of the Reformation. He wrote his wife, Katherine, "My heart has become cold, so that I do not like to be there any longer." He was aggravated that people seemed so indifferent to his preaching. Some even mocked him as they wondered aloud what gave Luther the right to question so much they had previously been taught.

"I am tired of this city and do not wish to return," he wrote. He would rather "eat the bread of a beggar than torture and upset my poor old age and final days with the filth at Wittenberg." Within a month, though, one of the town's citizens talked Luther into returning.

Though discouragement with preaching has been the common lot of preachers through the ages, there are some dynamics that make preaching a unique challenge as we enter the twenty-first century. Television seems to have co-opted people's attention spans. Relativism knocks the legs out from under authoritative preaching. A thousand modern Baals compete for people's loyalty. And our congregations, well, they continue to act like people: run-of-the-mill sinners.

It's enough to make a preacher want to go on strike. Or move.

Or learn how to make a difference despite the challenges.

Three preachers who have effectively met the challenge have come together to share their insights in this volume of Mastering Ministry's Pressure Points. As my colleagues David Goetz, Brian

Larson, Marshall Shelley, and I interviewed these gifted preachers and then edited those transcripts into the chapters you see here, we were impressed by the character of these men. None of them claims to have overcome discouragement; nor do any of them say they've figured out a flawless method to implant the gospel in resistant people. But each is widely known for his ability to communicate the Christian message creatively and cogently — and this in an age that, on the surface anyway, doesn't seem all that interested.

Steve Brown

Steve Brown can cope with the occasional wilderness of preaching because he's been through the deepest wilderness experience: when he began ministry, he wasn't a Christian, at least according to his own lights. He believed in a diluted, intellectual Christianity, he says. He had little confidence in the authority of Scripture, and he certainly didn't put much stock in the traditional doctrines of the church, like salvation by the cross, the dual nature of Christ, and so on.

At the time, he was serving a little church on Cape Cod, Massachusetts. Though he was an effective speaker, he says, "I didn't see any power in my life or ministry."

He met some Christians who had vibrant spiritual lives, and he was impressed, so he began to doubt his doubts. Still he held back. He said to a friend, "I still can't buy into all of this stuff. But I'm drawn by the warmth of these Christians. I just don't understand it. If I ever do understand, then I'll give myself to it."

Soon thereafter, he attended a retreat center, at which the sisters who ran the center would leave sayings and prayers on the pillows of the guests. When Steve arrived in his room and read the saying on his pillow, he was stunned: "My Father, I don't understand thee, but I trust thee."

Steve knew that needed to be his prayer. This became a turning point in his spiritual journey; he moved slowly from his spiritual wilderness into a vibrant, growing relationship with Christ.

This is one reason Steve's preaching is so well-received across the country, by Christians and skeptics alike. They see that he knows their struggles, doubts, and stretches of emptiness. They identify with his earthy, brash, contrarian manner.

Steve is president of Key Life Network, Inc., and Bible teacher on the national radio program, *Key Life*. He is also professor of communications and practical theology at Reformed Theological Seminary in Orlando, Florida. He formerly pastored Key Biscayne Presbyterian Church in Florida. His most recent book is *If Jesus Has Come: Thoughts on the Incarnation for Skeptics, Christians, and Christian Skeptics* (Baker).

Haddon Robinson

After an experience of a few years ago, Haddon Robinson is a new man and a new preacher. He was president of Denver Seminary, in Denver, Colorado, at the time, and because of his position, he was involved in two legal cases over the misconduct of two individuals associated with the school.

"It was the toughest experience I've ever gone through," he said. "When you have people pounding at your motives for eight or nine hours in a deposition, it hooks into any insecurities you have and magnifies them. I would read some of the Psalms where David says, 'I'm righteous.' Well, I came to the place where I wasn't sure I was righteous, where I doubted whether I had done the right thing in regard to these individuals. I became aware of my own terrible vulnerability, my inability to handle stress in a triumphantly faithful way. As a result, I began to be a believer in grace as never before."

During this time, as one of today's most respected preachers, he was scheduled for many speaking engagements: "I would go to preach, but I wouldn't feel like being there. I'd stand in the pulpit and feel unworthy: *Who are you to tell these people about living by faith when your faith is hardly vibrant right now!* There were times I thought, *I'll never preach again.*"

Haddon has since come through that experience, so he knows the struggles that preachers go through when their lives are a wilderness. And he brings wisdom and humility to the insights he shares.

Haddon now holds the Harold J. Ockenga chair of preaching at Gordon-Conwell Theological Seminary in South Hamilton, Massachusetts. He is author of *Biblical Preaching* (Baker) and editor of *Biblical Sermons: How Twelve Preachers Apply the Principles of Biblical Preaching* (Baker). He also is co-author of *Mastering Contemporary Preaching* (Multnomah).

William Willimon

William Willimon had an experience early in ministry that shook him into reality:

"One of the attractions of the parish ministry for me was that I liked to be liked. I loved to be loved. I'd had good luck at this undertaking: I was president of my class for many years running; you don't do that without being nice.

"Then I served my first church — surprise! Despite my charming personality (!), two families left my church. They said, 'We don't like the RSV Bible, we don't like preachers with long hair, and we don't like graduates of Emory University.' I thought at the time, sarcastically, *Well, only one of those is a good reason for leaving the church!*

"But this came as a great shock to me, that I couldn't get some people in the church to like me. And that does something to you."

In particular, that's done at least two things to Will. First, it's made him a bold preacher. He quickly figured out that not only is it impossible to please people, it's not what he was called to do. He concluded that, like their Lord, preachers have to bring a sword as much as they bring peace; we have to give up the desire to be liked if we're going to be faithful.

But Will doesn't leave it there. For he's also learned how to be a persuasive preacher. Though he doesn't pander, neither is he cavalier. He wants people to put their full trust in Christ, and his preaching is known for its ability to challenge people, in a compelling way, to do just that.

Will is dean of the chapel and professor of Christian ministry at Duke University in Durham, North Carolina. He has served

United Methodist pastorates in Georgia and South Carolina. His many books include *Preaching to Strangers: Evangelism in Today's World* (Westminster/John Knox) and *Peculiar Speech: Preaching to the Baptized* (Eerdmans).

The Virtues of a Good Preacher

Martin Luther once said, "A good preacher should have these properties and virtues: first, to teach systematically; secondly, he should have a ready wit; thirdly, he should be eloquent; fourthly, he should have a good voice; fifthly, a good memory; sixthly, he should know when to make an end; seventhly, he should be sure of his doctrine; eighthly, he should venture and engage body and blood, wealth and honor, in the Word; ninthly, he should suffer himself to be mocked and jeered of every one."

Luther had most, if not all, of these virtues, particularly the last — otherwise he couldn't have continued as long as he did in the pulpit.

Though few of us are openly mocked and jeered these days, we do know subtle and severe forms of discouragement and loneliness. In this volume, you'll find refreshing insights that will invigorate your preaching, whether your preaching ministry happens to feel like a dry wilderness or a lush garden.

— *Mark Galli*
contributing editor
LEADERSHIP

PART ONE
Culture Wars

Lives are changed through mere words — maybe that's the only way we ever change.

— *William Willimon*

CHAPTER ONE
The Power of Mere Words

When I was in graduate school at Emory, a fellow student developed a questionnaire for his congregation to measure their racial attitudes. He passed out a survey and recorded the results. Then he preached a series of five sermons that in some way touched on the race issue.

After his sermon series, he surveyed their responses — they were three points more racist than before!

I was surprised back then but not today. On many days since, I've wondered if my words were impotent. Getting up to preach was like trying to put out a thousand-acre forest fire with a garden hose. How could my words possibly make a difference to a mother who just lost her newborn to SIDS, to the wife who can't get pregnant, to the woman whose husband beats her regularly, to the chronically unemployed husband and father of five?

Furthermore, how can one person standing alone and speaking from an ancient book possibly impact this word-saturated, image-driven society? It seems impossible.

Yet according to Scripture, this is our chief weapon: words. So over the years, I've given this paradox a great deal of thought. Here is what I've discovered.

Insignificant Words

The office of pastor doesn't seem to be valued by society. We don't make a lot of money. We perform no specific function that directly contributes to the Gross National Product or index of leading economic indicators. The profession of clergy is usually right next to garbage collector on the list of most-valued careers by high school students.

No wonder we sometimes doubt the power of the preached word! We're not paranoid, then, when we begin to wonder about our preaching. Yet there are other reasons to wonder.

First, we feel we're up against Tom Brokaw, Dan Rather, and Peter Jennings. We believe our people expect us to preach like news anchors. They smoothly present the six o'clock evening news, speaking to us as if they were in our living rooms; that has heightened expectations. Few of us, however, can present God's Word with the same polish.

Second, we can never count on the Holy Spirit to move people as we expect. I have to live with the thought that some Sundays, the Holy Spirit might say, "Oh, by the way, Will, I'm working in Poland this week" — that's one reason I keep stomach medicine in the Duke Chapel bathroom.

I can work hard crafting my message, making my words coherent, and deliver these finely crafted words in a well-modulated voice, only to see it all fall on deaf ears. But then when I have little time for preparation and I breathe a prayer of desperation as I step into the pulpit, someone will say later, "One of the greatest contributions to my deciding to become a missionary was a sermon you preached." When I review which sermon that was, I invariably remember a Sunday when I felt disgusted with my performance.

Third, we feel overwhelmed with the reigning issues of the day; our message, frankly, feels irrelevant sometimes.

The Sunday after the last election, I preached a sermon on Christians and politics. The lectionary dictated the subject: the exchange between the Pharisees and Jesus about Caesar's coin.

"I want to tell you how to vote in the upcoming election," I said. "Oh, that's right. You've already voted. Isn't this just typical of the church? We're always coming a little late to the party."

I went on to explain that the morning's text was not written specifically to help Christians know how to behave toward government. "Luke says the Pharisees don't care one bit about Jesus' answer," I said. "They were trying to trap him. Jesus, as it turns out, is not all that interested in their question. He asks them, 'Whose picture is on the coin?' and then says, 'Well, Caesar must want it then.'

"Hey, people, this is a joke," I continued. "This text is supposed to be funny. Jesus is saying, 'If Caesar is desperate to have all this stuff, let him have it. But you be careful and give to God what is God's.' I don't know that Bill and Hillary are that important. I don't know that taxes are important. I think Jesus is after bigger fish than that."

I'm not saying the issues of our day should be ignored, but too often we let their seeming urgency overshadow the gospel, which in the end is the really urgent message we have.

Fourth, our words seem impotent sometimes because we rarely see our people change. An elderly woman in my last congregation said to me, "You should feel lucky to be here. Most churches would not put up with your preaching. I have Baptist friends who wouldn't take this; they would fire you. Fortunately for you, we Methodists have seen just about everything."

Apparently she had heard the Word preached for years but

had never seen fit to let it transform her. And it was clear my preaching wasn't having much of an impact.

So it's a tough environment in which we preach.

Afraid of the Power

I teach at Duke Divinity School, and from time to time my students bring in case studies of local church ministry. I've noticed some interesting patterns. One of them is lay people who report seeing a vision — hearing a word from God or a personal directive from Jesus while sitting on their patio, for example — and their clergy who don't believe them. The typical response of the clergy is, "Have you been working too hard? What did you have to eat last night?" Pastors are often the last to recognize the hand of God.

I've also noticed this pattern in Acts 12. Peter is jailed, and the local church at Jerusalem prays for his release. After being miraculously released, Peter walks to the house where a prayer meeting for his release is in progress. But those inside don't believe Rhoda, who insists it's Peter at the door.

"You're out of your mind," they tell her. They're shocked, in disbelief. Surely their prayers haven't been answered!

I'm tempted to react the same way when I think about the power of my words. Frankly, I'm unnerved by the effectiveness of the gospel, and sometimes I wish what I preached wasn't so powerful. First, I don't want to be responsible for people doing something "foolish." When an auto mechanic hears in my sermon a call to sell everything and become a missionary, I get nervous.

"Wait a minute. What are you doing?" I want to say. "I don't want this kind of power. This could be a disaster; you've got a wife and three small children and a mortgage. Someone could get hurt. I certainly don't want to hurt anybody."

Second, my pastoral side sometimes wants to shield my audience from the gospel's counter-cultural edge. From time to time, we invite the North Carolina legislature to Duke Chapel, and about half of them, including the governor and several on the North Carolina Supreme Court, show up.

On one of these occasions, I preached on repentance. I

mentioned that repentance was one of the weird things that Christians believe in, and that not everyone in our world believes in repentance. I talked about how saying, "I'm sorry," or "I was wrong; I apologize," is not a popular response of nations. I told the sad story of the Iranian airbus that was shot down accidentally by American missiles. I relayed the emotions I felt as I watched the footage of the tragedy on CNN — the bloated bodies of the victims bobbing in the ocean.

The moment I said that, my pastoral instincts chimed in, *This is going to hurt some feelings. These people came here for a nice celebration. Here I am, hitting them over the head with the gospel's implications.*

As it turned out, one newly elected legislator was deeply moved by the sermon and committed himself to legislating by his Christian convictions. Still, I'm sometimes nervous making the bold assertions the New Testament calls for.

Creating Worlds

We are right to be afraid of our words. They are powerful things. All of our worlds are linguistically constructed, that is, our worlds are built by words.

In Genesis 1 there is no world until God starts talking. When God does, stuff begins to happen. His words create a whole new world.

So do ours. A few years ago, my denomination published a magazine that focused on social action. The editors had interviewed leaders in our denomination who struggled for racial justice. One of the questions asked how they got to be leaders in this cause.

I was impressed by how many of those leaders mentioned preaching. As a result of hearing a sermon, they were motivated to pursue social action as their life's calling. A whole new world and lifestyle had opened up to them as a result of preaching.

Perhaps that's what the apostle Paul meant when he said, "Faith comes by hearing." Christian faith is auditorially derived. Lives are changed through mere words — maybe that's the only way we ever change.

The theological dynamic of this change — the work of the Holy

Spirit — is easy to understand, though somewhat of a nuisance.

I can think of many instances when after a sermon someone has walked up to me and said, "Thank you. This morning's sermon on salvation was so moving."

Salvation? I think. *This morning's sermon was not on salvation. It was on loving your neighbor!* The Holy Spirit had twisted my words and applied them in a way I didn't expect.

The Holy Spirit is also annoyingly unpredictable. Last summer I led a Bible study at a resort where my words had such a deadening effect that the summer help was dangerously close to being called in to drag the people out by their feet.

"Bear with me, folks," I begged. "I only have several paragraphs left." My forbearing listeners wept at this pronouncement. *Let me out of here, Lord,* I thought. *I promise never to come back here.*

I'd been there the year before leading a similar study. That time the air was electrified with the power of the Spirit. Stuff was happening. And when I ended, the room fell silent. Then applause broke out. Everyone felt the Spirit of God hover over the study.

I trace both effects to the Holy Spirit. The ways of the Holy Spirit may stump me, but that's what makes preaching such a wonderful adventure. The Holy Spirit converts preaching from a science into a beautiful art form, an art form that creates new worlds.

Letting the Word Emerge

So, the Word we preach is intrinsically powerful; by the working of the Holy Spirit, it creates new worlds. But it isn't as if we offer people just words, words in total isolation. When we preach, other dynamics are at work, and the more sensitive we are to them — the better we make use of these dynamics — the more the sermon's power can fully emerge.

For example, there is the love we have for our people. I once visited a church of one of our Duke Divinity School graduates and was severely embarrassed at his sermon. He had a virtual speech impediment. He tripped over every other sentence, repeated himself, and basically stumbled through the entire twenty-five minutes.

During the coffee time following the service, a woman walked up to me and said, "Boy, do we like Duke Divinity School! You people really do a job on clergy."

"Really?" I said. I wondered if she were joking.

"Oh yes," she replied. "We owe our preacher to you."

I was thinking that during the sermon! I thought.

"He has set this church on fire," she said. "Isn't it obvious to you?"

"Ah, no."

"It's his preaching!"

"His preaching?" I asked, staring in disbelief.

"Oh, it's so obvious that he has so much to say and finds putting these important things into words so difficult," she stated.

Wow! I thought. *What a beautiful testimony of the relationship between a congregation and its preacher. She loved him, and his words came across to her as meaningful.*

I served a church in North Myrtle Beach before coming to Duke, and I rarely got angry responses from my audience except from the visitors. Our church was located in a resort community, so our summer services were filled with visitors. I once preached on divorce, and the visitors lined up at the end of the service to gripe at me: "You're so insensitive! Don't you have divorced people in your congregation?"

I later realized why the visitors wouldn't put up with me: we had no relationship. With the regulars, I was the first person on the scene when trouble arose. When they went to court, I was there. If they contracted an illness, I was there to comfort them and their families. My congregation had given me authority to speak on difficult matters in a way the visitors hadn't.

Second, each of us has a God-given personality we bring to the pulpit. One student from the Midwest rarely uttered a word in class. One of the requirements of the class was to preach from the first ten chapters of Genesis. This quiet student chose to preach on the flood. When he preached, he read the story of the Garden of Eden and then the story of the flood. He opened with a slow-moving story about working in a summer camp where he met a young man who became his best friend.

He went on to describe their long walks in the woods, the beauty of the Wisconsin trees, and sitting on the mountainside.

Okay, I thought. *Get to the point. Where are you going with this?*

The student went on, "My friend invited me home with him, and we visited a small farm near where he lived. My friend said, 'Since you and I have gotten to be such good friends, I want to show you something very important to me.' We walked into his family's barn, which was filled with neo-Nazi posters, submachine guns, anti-Jewish literature, and other hate propaganda."

This student then pounded the pulpit and began preaching emotionally about what he saw there. He pointed out that in the Noah story some were saved, but the evil continues, and all God says is that he won't kill us again by water, though we richly deserve it. He ended by saying, "We are a people who need saving." Then he sat down.

The class was silent. Part of the sermon's power came from this student's honest use of his own personality. He was quiet and unemotional for the most part, but when something troubled him, he let us know.

Finally, we bring our bodies to the pulpit. The better our use of body language, the more effective our message.

A preaching professor at Duke used to play in his class a video of sermons collected from various preachers around the country. When one of the tv preachers said, "I want to talk to you about our financial needs," he would reach over, pick up his Bible, and open it to a passage. He never referred to the Bible directly. In fact, his point had nothing whatsoever to do with the Bible. He skillfully used symbols to move his audience to react a certain way.

After reviewing the video with his class, the professor would say, "I wish I could get you to be half as sensitive to gestures, to eye contact, to tone of voice as this media preacher."

He wasn't advocating manipulation. But our mannerisms can

get in the way of the Word, or, if used sensitively, they can amplify the power of our message.

Detonating the Dynamite

Recently a Duke student about to graduate knocked at my door.

"Dr. Willimon," he began, "one of your sermons saved my life. I was considering suicide until I heard you preach one Sunday. I just wanted to thank you before I left school for good."

"Wow! That's great," I replied. "When was this?"

"I think it was last January, the week after classes started up again. The sermon was the one on the love of God that is higher and deeper and wider than anything."

My mind was spinning; I couldn't remember preaching such a message. Then it hit me.

"Ah, wait a minute," I said. "Dr. Thomas Long preached that sermon, not me."

"Oh yeah," the student replied, "the guy with the blondish hair. Oh well, you two look a lot alike."

"Well, I'm glad you didn't take your life, and I'm sure Dr. Long would be thrilled."

I was a little miffed that I hadn't preached the sermon, but I was once again impressed with the life-changing power of the preacher's words.

Gerhard von Rad, a German Old Testament scholar, once said that the best sermon he ever heard was given in the middle of World War II — some of the darkest days for the Germans. With bombs exploding all around and fear striking the hearts of all Germans, this tiny congregation had gathered to hear a young inexperienced preacher. When he stood up to preach, he gingerly and carefully opened up the Bible to his text as if he were, von Rad said, unwrapping a package of dynamite.

Our words are not mere words. With them we unloose the powerful and wildly unpredictable truths of the gospel, transforming lives in the here and now — and forever.

Our listeners know us, trust us, and see in us lives that largely back up what we preach. That accomplishes more than mere homiletical skills ever can.

— Haddon Robinson

Competing with the Communication Kings

Your sermon ends, and you're pleased with it. Then someone from the congregation approaches with a beaming smile.

"Nice sermon, Pastor. Say, did you hear Charles Stanley on television this morning? He has been preaching on grace for several weeks. Powerful messages! He says that . . ."

The church member means well, but you can't help but feel people are comparing you — unfavorably — with someone who is a ten-talent preacher, a communication king.

When I was in seminary, celebrated preachers spoke in our

chapel and at local conferences: Harry Ironside, Vernon McGee, Roy Aldrich, Stephen Olford, Ray Stedman. After hearing these preachers, others were inspired. But I walked out of the service wanting to quit. I remember once reading a sermon by Peter Marshall and literally weeping in frustration because I could not produce a sermon approaching his. Reading a communication king made me want to get out of preaching altogether.

Many pastors can identify with those feelings. Today many more "kings" rule the homiletical landscape. Media preachers are some of the most gifted, and they enjoy extra advantages like researchers, audio or video engineers, and freedom from the drain of everyday pastoring.

In addition, local pastors preach in the communication age. Every day of the week, our people hear the best communication money can buy, from smooth TV newspeople, to dazzling entertainers, to hilarious comedians—all of whom are supplied with words by professional wordsmiths. Madison Avenue spends millions on thirty-second TV spots or one-page magazine ads that communicate with allure and power.

How have the communication kings affected the expectations people have for the preaching of the local pastor? In basketball, a dunk used to be a novelty, but now even the guards "play above the rim." Have the communication kings raised the level of play required of everyone? Does the local pastor have any advantages over communication kings? Are communication kings friends or competitors? What can we learn from them?

Jarred Judgment

We have to admit it: communication kings are skilled and talented. And they are good in the very field we've given our lives to. It's only natural for a pastor to feel intimidated.

We mustn't blow this out of proportion, however—which is precisely what preachers, given our make-up, are tempted to do. A pastor's soul is sensitive. All well and good, but the dark side is pastors tend to be more thin-skinned about slights and criticism. If twenty-five parishioners say, "Good sermon" to the pastor on their way out of church and one woman half-kiddingly says, "Well, there's always next week," we spend the rest of the afternoon wondering what she meant by that.

Two experiences of my own illustrate this hypersensitivity, which can cause us to doubt and sometimes misread the effect of our preaching.

Several years ago, I spoke at a youth workers convention, but I felt the message went poorly. When I used a key illustration out of place, it put me off balance. I had that sensation of mentally stepping outside myself and thinking about how badly my sermon was going even as I preached it. I noticed a few young people reading magazines.

When I finished, I felt the sermon had bombed, and I just wanted to escape the building.

Several months later, I was chatting with a couple of people who had been at the convention, who said, "We really appreciated your message." Assuming they were just being kind, I brushed off their comments.

Six months later still, I was packing for a trip and grabbed a handful of sermon tapes to listen to on the plane. The next day, as I rummaged through the tapes, I noticed that I had inadvertently grabbed the sermon from the youth convention, a message I had no intention of listening to again. But I changed my mind, and with a slight cringe, I put it in the tape player.

I was stunned. I had said what I had wanted to say in the sermon, and I felt I had said it well. Now that several months had passed, I could listen objectively. My feelings while preaching that sermon had not conformed to reality.

Of course, it works both ways. On another occasion, I spoke at a church and felt the sermon was a tremendous success. After the service, as I was waiting in the back of the sanctuary for the pastor, I noticed a pew card someone had written on. I read it with some dismay: "I wonder how long this guy's going to preach. There's going to be a long line at the cafeteria."

Obviously my sermon had not had much impact on this unknown scribbler.

The point is this: our high sensitivity to the effectiveness of our preaching sometimes jars our immediate judgment. And in relation to the communication kings, it puts us immediately on the defensive. When we recognize that, it already begins to relieve some of the pressure we feel. But there's more.

The Advantages of the Local Pastor

Although those who preach to national audiences via TV, radio, tapes, and conferences have a lot going for them, the local pastor also has some huge advantages. We're playing on a more level field than we imagine.

We benefit, first, from a personal, loving relationship with our listeners. When we stand in the pulpit, we have the credibility and spiritual authority that comes only from having been with people in their times of need. When we preach on the power of prayer, parishioners know us as the pastors who have interceded with them when they were unemployed. When we preach on compassion, they know us as preachers who have wept with them at the funeral home.

Our listeners know us, trust us, and see in us lives that largely back up what we preach. That example accomplishes more than mere homiletical skills ever can.

The local pastor also enjoys the advantage of local accent. Listeners quickly pick up when a speaker is an outsider.

I once heard a preacher use a baseball illustration by saying, "The batter got a four-base hit." People use the terms *two-base hit* and *three-base hit*, but anyone who knows baseball would say the batter hit a home run. The speaker, it turned out, was not American.

What's true on a national level is even more true at the local level. There are many local "accents" that only the local pastor can appreciate and use to advantage.

Language accents. In some parts of the country, people say *supper* for the evening meal; in others *dinner* is the word. Some towns use *pop* and others *soda* when referring to soft drinks. In New England we call milk shakes, *freezes*. Some regions speak more slowly, with a twang or drawl, others at a clipped rate. In the West, people say, "I'm going with you." In the Midwest, they say, "I'm going with."

The preacher naturally adapts to such nuances, and thus identifies with people in a way national TV preachers cannot.

Social accents. In a blue-collar town, people tend to use rougher vernacular, and they usually disdain bookish language. They are suspicious of experts; instead, they respect common people and their common sense.

In a middle-class, college-educated suburb, people value higher education and use more abstract speech. They often defer to experts, and they respect sophistication.

The local pastor can tune his or her sermon to reflect these social accents. Furthermore, the local preacher can refer to town jokes or mention the nicknames for significant landmarks and buildings in the area.

For instance, in the Chicago area, "The El" is shorthand for one of the local commuter train systems, and "Metra" is the name for the other. By simply referring to one or the other in an illustration, the pastor will have set a scene that locals can identify with.

Historical accents. The local pastor knows the events significant to residents: the big fire, the great flood, the high-school basketball championship year. A local pastor can say, "I read the obituary for Coach Peterson in the paper yesterday. You all knew him. He taught history to most of your children. He was a stalwart in our community, who inspired young people. He reminds us how vibrant and alive someone can be, and how quickly death comes."

A local illustration like that affects a congregation more profoundly than quoting Aristotle or Byron on death.

All these accents give the local pastor a rapport, a trust, the advantage of being an insider, someone who knows the people.

Thomas Long, professor of preaching at Princeton Theological Seminary, once said that great preaching these days is local, that is, it arises out of and makes reference to local events, local language, and local people. The communication kings may have a national following, but local preachers who can speak with the unique accents of their people can have a stronger impact.

Partners and Mentors

We do have advantages then. Still, the communication kings influence our congregations significantly, and we cannot pretend otherwise. We don't have to respond with insecurity and defensiveness though. Here are two positive responses that may help you take advantage of their ministries.

● *Be grateful.* It's natural to be jealous of the great preachers, though we rarely recognize jealousy as such. It usually takes the form of carping criticism of their ministries whenever their names are mentioned.

Communication kings attract jealousy like a picnic attracts ants. In a culture that honors individualism and competition, great communicators seem to have more "success" in ministry. And if someone else wins, we assume we have lost.

It doesn't have to be that way. A friend who pastors in Denver is learning to get over jealousy. Some time ago, a number of people left his church and started attending a nearby megachurch. He struggled with resentment and anger for several days. He decided his only hope was prayer, so he began praying for the megachurch and its pastor. He regularly prayed, "Thank you, God, that they are touching people we could never reach."

His attitude turned around. Thereafter, when he heard about successes of the megachurch, he could rejoice because his prayers were being answered. His praying helped him realize his church and the megachurch were on the same team, part of a larger network. When the bigger church succeeded, the team succeeded.

He's also learned to express that attitude from the pulpit. Publicly praying for "rival" preachers teaches a congregation and reinforces for the pastor the idea that small ministries aren't competing with large.

In a similar way, if a parishioner says, "I really get a lot out of Charles Stanley's sermons. You ought to watch him," we can respond, "Isn't it wonderful the way God has given these gifts to

Charles Stanley and how he's reaching so many people?" It sounds corny, but it's an old idea, and a biblical idea, and I've discovered it works. We can rejoice with those who rejoice.

The highest goal of team members is to win. The woman who swims the second lap in the relay is grateful that her teammate took the final lap in record time. Rivalry — and thus jealousy — isn't the issue. The gold medal is, and so gratefulness is her usual attitude.

● *Imitate strengths — not weaknesses.* The Michael Jordans of the preaching world inspire us to, as the commercial says, "wanna be like Mike." Easier said than done. Ironically, what pastors often imitate are the communication king's idiosyncrasies and weaknesses.

Communication kings succeed *despite* their weaknesses, not because of them. But their idiosyncrasies are so visible, that's what those who imitate them pick up on.

One prominent preacher had the habit of gesturing a phrase too late. He'd say, "It was a wide, wide desert," and then a half-second later, he'd spread his arms wide. With him it never distracted; his strengths overcame his problem. Dozens of his followers, however, now gesture late, and it looks like a cheap imitation.

Another celebrated preacher shakes his leg whenever he gets wired up. For him, that's an endearing mannerism. But when those trained by him do the same thing, it looks as though they have a nerve disease.

Some successful preachers of the past loudly sucked air or said, "Amen," between virtually every sentence. Many have imitated them, to their detriment.

In order to learn from the strengths of great preachers, we need to listen to one of their sermons three or four times. It takes that many hearings to get some emotional distance from the sermon and analyze what the speaker is doing.

First, try to understand what the sermon does well and then ask why. Does it affect your emotions in an authentic way? Compel your interest in the introduction? End with a great sense of resolution and inspiration? Why are the main points so memorable? What gave the sermon authority?

In addition to analyzing sermons, we can profit from the

continuing study of homiletics, which provides us with the categories we need to analyze what effective communicators do.

For example, my continuing study of preaching books and articles has helped me see how modern listeners have evolved. Modern listeners respond well to an inductive approach to sermons, where a number of examples from life are given and then principles extracted from them. Listeners are a bit bored when we begin by expounding principles, even if the principles are illustrated. Many modern hearers prefer to explore a subject and discover answers along with the preacher, rather than simply being told the conclusions.

Once I became aware of this pattern in modern communication, I was able to notice how effective communicators exploited it successfully.

Every year I choose a different noted preacher, some living and others from the past — Peter Marshall, Charles Finney, Alexander Maclaren — and study him for a full year. I read his sermons and his biography. If possible, I listen to or view tapes of his sermons. I read anything I can find about how he prepared sermons. Then when I get stumped in the middle of writing a sermon, I can ask myself, "How would Spurgeon have handled this? What would Clovis Chappell do to make this live?"

I also study secular communication kings to figure out their approaches. I was watching John Bradshaw, a pop psychologist who talks about relationships and the inner child. I concluded that part of Bradshaw's popularity stems from his talking to people about people. I wondered, *Does simply applying the Bible to people make people feel preached at? Does talking about their lives from the Bible, using the Scriptures as a way to explain their experiences, their struggles, and then bringing in the Bible's solutions help them listen?* That's a subtle difference that may have a major effect on how secular listeners respond.

One characteristic of great athletes is they can make everyone around them play better. They aren't just stars; they make ordinary players into a star team.

The communication kings may have made me feel insecure

and at times inadequate, but I'm a better preacher today because of them. Their examples have inspired, challenged, and instructed me. We may not all play above the rim, but they've elevated our games, helping each of us to make the most of the one, two, or ten "talents" God has given us. We're not competing against the communication kings; we're competing with them.

If an apparently strong-willed pastor admits struggles from the pulpit, it becomes a powerful preaching moment.

— *Steve Brown*

CHAPTER THREE

Voice of Authority or Fellow Struggler?

Our church had just signed a contract for a $3 million building project. I panicked when those I banked on to help pay for it refused.

So I called up every elder and deacon and cajoled them to pledge towards the project. I recruited someone to paste a large picture of our church on a cardboard box and cut it up into bricks of $10,000 each. I also convinced the elders and deacons to stand in front of the church one Sunday and announce their 100 percent support for the project.

Then, as a climax to all my work, I preached a hard-sell message, a the-time-for-fun-and-games-is-over sermon.

It didn't work. We raised the money, all right, but in the meantime I was criticized severely. I so deeply offended one person, he left the church. And that upset his girlfriend terribly, because she had decided to stay!

As I look back, I realize how manipulative the sermon was. I practically said that if people didn't give they would get the fever! The church at that moment didn't need a blistering prophet who threatened but a gentle pastor who encouraged. In retrospect, I should have identified with people: "This is a huge goal, and even I'm afraid to make the sacrifices required to fulfill it. But if we depend on God, he can give us courage to do it together."

I've been wrong in the other direction, as well, being vulnerable when I should have kicked the congregation in the seat of the pants!

This is one of the toughest problems the modern pastor faces. We are called to be heralds of the truth, yet if we don't do that well, it backfires. People today don't like to be told what to do or what to believe.

People need and want to hear how a pastor shares their struggles and pain. Nonetheless, a part of them longs to hear an authoritative word to guide their lives.

Different preachers bring different gifts to the pulpit. Some are proclaimers, with an authoritative word. Others are more intimate: "Let me tell you what God has been doing in my life." Naturally, we should major in our strengths.

Still, for most preachers in most settings, we need to do both if we hope to offer God's Word in a way that affects people deeply. It has taken me years to learn to do both well, and I'm still learning. Here are some principles I keep in mind.

A Strong Foundation

When a weak pastor admits to struggling in the faith, the congregation hardly takes notice. That's pretty much what they expect, given how feebly he or she has been leading the church. But if an apparently strong-willed pastor admits struggles from the pulpit, it becomes a powerful preaching moment.

That's one reason I believe the preacher should, first and foremost, be a proclaimer of God's Word. In the long run, it gives us authority when we preach with authority *and* when we preach as a fellow struggler.

But another reason is more critical: preachers are under obligation to God's truth. We are handlers of Holy Scripture, which bestows upon us the authority to herald its teachings. In doing so, there's no getting around the fact that we're in a league of our own, different from that of the listener.

Consequently, no matter what style we'll emphasize, we need first to establish ourselves as strong, authoritative pastors. Years ago, a pastor friend of mine gave me an insight into pastoring:

"Steve, people look at us as representatives of God. I don't like this, and it's not biblical. But the way they treat us is the way they feel they can treat God. So if you allow people to walk over you, they think they can do that to God."

Maybe I liked it because I instinctively have operated that way.

When I arrived at one church, I was young and ambitious, and the church asked me to target the youth; the church was slowly graying. So I began developing relationships with the teenagers in the church neighborhood. The basketball hoop in the church parking lot turned out to be an effective means of getting next to them.

I had served the church for only six months when one evening the chairman of the trustee board nonchalantly mentioned to me, as we were standing under the basketball hoop, that the board had decided to remove the hoop.

I exploded. "No, you're not! By taking down that basketball hoop, you're sending a strong message to those kids. You asked me to attract young people here, but you'll be running them off."

The chairman waved me off, pivoted, and walked away from me.

I was livid. "Jack, don't walk away from me!"

He kept walking, but I persisted. I followed him up two flights of stairs smack into the middle of a trustee meeting. I sat down.

"Don't worry," Jack said to the other trustees. "Pastor and I are just having a little disagreement."

Then he added, "By the way, I've invited the pastor to come to our meeting." (Pastors were normally excluded from the trustees' meeting.)

"Could I say something, Jack?" I asked. I paused and then turned to face the entire board.

"First, Jack didn't invite me to this meeting. I'm the pastor of this church and don't need an invitation to a trustee meeting. Second, I will be at these trustee meetings from now on."

The air was heavy with silence, and I went on to complain about the backboard decision. But I had gained their respect. I can't lay claim to knowing consciously what I was doing, but in effect I was building a base of strength, from which I could operate in the proclamation mode on Sunday morning.

Gaining Authority

It is critical to establish authority. This is especially important for young pastors or pastors in new church settings. If they are going to have any success in the pulpit, their authority must be established early and maintained regularly. But how do we do that?

One way, though it must be handled as carefully as removing asbestos, is by picking one issue a year — an issue big enough to resign over — and push the conflict to a head.

Once, I switched job responsibilities of several of the church staff. I relayed my plans to the session, expecting them to approve officially my actions, as they usually did with staff issues.

I was wrong. First they said they wanted to think about it; then they became increasingly negative. The issue ballooned into an all-out power struggle.

I decided this was a "resignable issue," so I called a special session.

I opened the meeting boldly: "I'm not going to take responsibility for what happens in this church without authority to make staff decisions. If the staff begins to think I don't have the authority to hire, fire, and organize the staff as I see fit, I can't do what you want me to do. We're going to decide right now what we're going to do about this!"

After some discussion, one of them (who had initially balked at my changes) said, "Steve, we don't care how you arrange the staff. But if you don't want our input, don't ask us what we think."

Out of that we worked out a new set of agreements on our roles in the church.

I hated that meeting. The thought of confronting the board ate away at me, and I thought I was going to lose control at the meeting. I tried to talk myself out of it: *I'm not going to make any waves over this.* But then I realized how much of my leadership would be sacrificed if I didn't make waves. It takes a lot out of you, but sometimes you have to do it.

Though the incident had nothing to do with preaching, it buttressed my overall credibility as a leader, and that naturally increased my authority in the pulpit.

Another way to convey more authority is to become sensitive to the symbols of authority.

When I entered ministry, I *looked* young. I knew I would have trouble preaching authoritatively if people thought of me as baby faced. So I grew a beard. That helped.

Some pastors don robes (if their tradition permits it); others install larger pulpits. In any case, we are wise to make wise use of such symbols.

If a strength of ours communicates authority, we need to highlight it. My voice is naturally deep, so I made sure I kept it in the bass range to compensate for my youth.

Actually, that voice, when heard only over the radio, makes me bigger than life to some people. Recently, an elderly woman approached Kathy, my assistant at Key Life Network, after a rally at which I had spoken.

"I had to come this evening," she said. "I wanted to see what Steve looked like." She had heard me for some time over the radio.

"Well, was he what you expected?" Kathy replied.

"No," she said. "I expected the Marlboro man, and I was greatly disappointed."

Finally, from time to time you can reassert your authority by simply grabbing people by the collar and shaking them: "This is important. Listen. This is from God." I do that a lot.

Key Qualification

Of course, a million qualifications crowd my mind as I make these suggestions. Power can be dangerously abused, or spouting off foolishly can wind up losing you all credibility, even getting you fired.

But the biggest qualification is this: you've got to earn the right to confront, or even to use the symbols of authority. And that means sacrificial pastoral care is required.

One pastor I know is the very image of strength and authority. At staff meetings he bluntly holds staff members accountable for their duties:

"I asked you to contact six visitors this week. Did you do it?"

"And I asked you to get cards out to all seniors? Did you do it?"

"Now this week, this is what I expect from each of you . . ."

He's a no-nonsense leader. But I once found out why he gets away with it.

He asked me to speak at his church one Sunday. One of his members picked me up from the airport, and on the drive to the church, I asked the driver what he thought of his pastor.

"I don't like him."

"Really?" I said.

"Yeah," he replied. "But don't get me wrong. I'll follow him to the pit of hell."

I became curious and asked why.

"When my mother was dying," the man said, "he didn't leave her side for forty-eight hours."

This pastor had earned his authority.

When It's Time to Get Intimate

I'm not a naturally warm person, and in some pastoral situations that has been a problem.

When I first arrived at Key Biscayne Presbyterian Church, I developed a friendship with a man who launched *Dolphin* magazine. Three months before he died, he made a decision to follow Christ. The night before he died, he said, "Steve, a lot of people don't know that I've found faith in Jesus Christ. So when you're standing over my casket, I want you to tell those attending my funeral what happened to me and how it can happen to them."

The church was packed the day of his funeral, and I preached an evangelistic message, keeping my promise to him. Afterwards, everybody was hugging and consoling his widow. She walked over to me at one point and gave me a hug. I hugged her, but I must have winced because she said, "Are you angry?"

"Ginny, not at all," I said. "I love you a lot, but I'm just not comfortable with hugging yet."

Now, years later, no one would believe this of me. I come across to many as someone who could be anyone's best friend. But this is something I've learned.

Though I'm a dyed-in-the-wool proclaimer, I'm also communication driven. I'm a teacher. I'm driven to help people understand what I'm saying. I long to make Jesus Christ real to people.

And I've learned that if I'm going to communicate with the modern world, I'm going to have to be as much fellow struggler as herald of God's Word. Still, I must admit that I began learning this by default.

Several years ago, I developed a terrible pain in my hip, so bad that for almost a year I was forced to walk with a cane. I couldn't even stand up to preach. Every time I'd lean in a certain direction, a searing pain would shoot through my body.

But I still had to preach — that was my livelihood. So I found a bar stool, and with microphone and Bible in hand, I preached sitting in front of the church. Right before the sermon, someone would move the pulpit aside and replace it with this stool that swiveled.

The move from the pulpit to the chair, I discovered, increased my effectiveness. The symbol of the big pulpit served only to accentuate my natural tendencies as a proclaimer. When that was removed, many in my church remarked that I had become less preachy. Instead of communicating, "This is the way it is," my sermons subtly shifted to "Can we talk together this morning?"

So just as symbols can communicate authority, they can also communicate intimacy.

Also, if you want to communicate intimacy, few things are more effective than simply telling the congregation you care about them.

I had a pastor friend who told me, "I'm in trouble in my church, and I don't know what to do." After some conversation, I concluded that although Bill loved his congregation, he had yet to communicate it to them. He gives you the impression he wants to be left alone; he has a natural scowl on his face. But it belies his real feelings.

So I told him, "Bill, you need to say from the pulpit, 'Guys, I know I look like I'm mad at you all the time, and I know you don't think I like you. But I think you're the best thing since sliced bread. I feel so privileged to be your pastor. I love you.' If you'd say that one time, you wouldn't be in trouble any longer."

Another help is the counsel of friends. One of my pastor friends has always been a strong proclaimer, partly because he looks like a movie star, partly because he's naturally arrogant. He knows arrogance is a problem. So some time ago, he said to his elders, "I know I'm arrogant, and I struggle with it all the time. I don't like that about myself. I want you guys to help me with this."

He never said this from the pulpit — that would have been to throw his authority out the window — but it was a winsome thing to do. It not only convinced his board that he was a fellow struggler, it gave my friend some periodic feedback about what he was communicating from the pulpit.

Finally, I need to make sure I know who I am. I'm a sinner. And I'm a sufferer. And when I suffer, I want to make sure I drink the full cup of it, so that I can learn what God is teaching me. Most of all, I want to make sure I experience grace.

Then whatever I say from the pulpit comes out okay. I don't come across as insensitive to people's situations. Nor do I seem like a pitiful wimp who knows nothing of God's victory. I can communicate I understand while proclaiming God's truth.

Mistakes to Avoid

In becoming more vulnerable from the pulpit, we become vulnerable to some homiletic mistakes. Here are three I especially try to avoid.

First, I don't want to lose it. Though I want to show people I too have emotions, I don't want to lose control.

Walter was my father figure, whose gentle wisdom and love guided me through a morass of hatred and division that I stepped into at one church.

The church was a war zone — father against son, husband against wife — before and after I arrived. Actual fistfights had broken out in the narthex, which were reported in several of the Boston newspapers. The most divisive issue was the placement of the Communion table in the new sanctuary. In fact, when I candidated there, the search committee asked me, "Where would you put a Communion table?"

I, not knowing the significance of the issue, naively replied, "You can hang it from the ceiling for all I care." My smart-aleck answer got me the job. I was hired and then baptized into an ugly church fight.

Walter and I prayed together almost every day before he contracted cancer. The night he died, I visited him in the hospital. He begged me to stay with him a little longer, but I had another obligation. The doctors told me he would be fine, so I left, promising Walter I would see him in the morning.

I would never again see him alive, however; Walter slipped away in the night. I was devastated. I had just lost my one pillar in what seemed to be a house of cards.

Three days later, I presided over Walter's funeral. And during the service, I fell apart. I would start to cry, and the organ would begin playing softly. Then I'd sit down until I regained composure. I'd stand up again, only to lose it again. Walter's death opened up within me a floodgate of emotion.

When the service finally ended, several people commented, "It was obvious you loved Walter," and "Your tears showed the depth of your feelings." They identified with my loss; I had mourned alongside them.

But I had failed as their pastor. I owed the family a service that would glorify God and comfort them in their mourning. Certainly it's appropriate to tell people how badly you feel, and even a tear or two is okay. But I have to remember I'm the pastor called on to do more than simply share my feelings.

Second, I don't want to over-tell. Once we've found a crisis in our lives, it's tempting to retell it whenever we can to help listeners see that we know about crises.

A recent crisis for my wife and me came our way from the ocean: Hurricane Andrew. We found ourselves huddled in a small closet as the winds blasted South Miami. We believed our deaths were imminent. In the end, we lost our home and many of our possessions but not each other.

This was too good a story not to tell. So I did, again and again as the opportunity presented itself. Three months later, I was speaking at a gathering of leaders in Colorado Springs when it suddenly struck me that for the last three months I had relayed our story at every place I had spoken. Enough was enough, I concluded.

Third, I don't want to get specific about some sins. Though we want to communicate that we're sinners, it's not always appropriate to go into details. Otherwise we undermine people's confidence.

Some sins, like my anger, I'm free to describe in detail — just as I've told stories in this chapter. Other sins, though, I talk about only in a general way. When preaching about greed, for instance, I might say, "With this sin I've prayed, 'Forgive me my sins,' " or "I've got a problem with this sin, but if you think I'm going to be detailed about it, you're crazy!" So, in one statement I can let people know I'm human, without being inappropriate.

The Intimate Herald

Many years ago, I spoke at a Youth for Christ retreat. I did everything I could, short of standing on my head, to communicate to those teenagers, but the entire front row of boys slept through the entire weekend of services. So later, when asked to speak at a large convention of teenagers, I initially refused: once bitten, twice shy. I wasn't keen on a repeat performance, but I eventually though reluctantly accepted the invitation.

That evening, after the band finished their set, I got up to speak to an auditorium full of teenagers. Someone had left a stool on stage, so I sat down, adjusted my half-glasses, and opened my big black Bible to the evening's text.

Suddenly the room fell silent. The students listened almost breathlessly, hanging on my every word. I was not a little surprised, to say the least, considering the reaction of my last teenage audience.

As I reflect upon the dynamics of that evening, part of the effect, I believe, was my gray hair, my deep voice, and my sitting down in front of them. All of that combined to have some sort of guru effect on the audience. I became the intimate herald, one who identified with them yet who spoke a word from the Lord.

I urge preachers not to violate their personalities. We are most effective at what makes each of us unique: our gifts and abilities. Some of us will naturally lean more toward proclamation, others at being a warm, charismatic witness of God's truth. Yet I'm convinced that each of us, when we're preaching at our best, can employ both to great effect.

Part Two

Internal Pressures

If people don't take the preacher seriously, they are not likely to take the message seriously.

— *Steve Brown*

CHAPTER FOUR

When You're Not Taken Seriously

O ne of my pastor friends and his wife attended his wife's twentieth high school reunion. His wife later reported to him that as she was talking to an old friend, catching up on their lives, she mentioned she had married a pastor.

As soon as the words were out, a look of pain crossed her friend's face.

"I'm so sorry," her friend said, her voice softening to a whisper. "I'm sorry because sex is *sooo* wonderful."

Perceptions like this make me angry. People tend to see

pastors as nice people who say nice things to nice people. We certainly don't know anything about the real world! We've become irrelevant in many people's eyes.

And whatever form it takes, I take it personally. Nothing ruffles my feathers more than being dismissed or patronized. I'd rather preach to an audience that's angry at me than one that thinks all I do is carry a black umbrella and attend women's teas.

I've had to come to terms with this fact about our culture, including much of the church culture: often we pastors aren't taken seriously. That's a problem not because of who I am, but because of who I represent. If people don't take me, the preacher, seriously, they are not likely to take my message seriously.

So I've done more than come to terms with this fact; I've also learned how to fight it.

Reasons for Disrespect

We should begin by noticing a few of the reasons we're not taken seriously. Some reasons, of course, have deep social or spiritual roots. These we can't do anything about.

For instance, I'm convinced many dismiss us because of a supernatural struggle in their lives. After I had written my first book, I was interviewed by a radio station in Boston. With five minutes left in the interview, I realized I had talked about myself the entire time. So I immediately switched to the subject of Christ and attempted to communicate the essence of the gospel during the remaining moments.

Afterwards, several of the cameracrew and the taping director surrounded me and began firing questions at me about the Christian faith. I answered their questions until everyone except the director was gone.

I suddenly remembered I had an appointment. "Look, let me give you my card," I said to him. "I'll write the name of a couple of books on the back of it. Call me after you read these books. Then we'll sit down and talk again."

"Thanks, Reverend," he said.

As I walked out of the studio, pushing open its swinging doors, the director called out, "Hey, Reverend!" I turned around. "I don't think I'm going to read these books," he said.

"Why not? You're asking questions," I replied.

"Yeah, you're right. But I don't want to read them. Because if I read them, I may find out you're right. And if you're right, I've got to change. But I don't want to change."

Rarely are people as honest as this director or even self-aware enough to know why they dismiss our preaching. But at least he respected the messenger. A lot of people dismiss us preachers because if they took us seriously they would have to take our message seriously. We have no control over whether they are ready to do that.

Still, there are many issues over which I do have some control, and the reason I'm not getting respect is because I'm not acting as if I deserve it. Here are two.

1. We take ourselves too seriously. A pastor friend in California tells the story of the time he was playing golf with several men, one of whom was a pastor. On the ninth hole, this pastor sliced the ball into the rough and exclaimed, "Damn!"

My friend can't resist the opportunity to needle, so he said sarcastically, "Pastor Greg, I can't believe a pastor would say something like that!"

The pastor was taken aback, and he stammered, "I'm so sorry. That was so unlike me."

"Hold on. I was just kidding you," my friend replied. But it was too late. This pastor was unnerved for the rest of the afternoon.

We're sometimes so concerned about being a model of Christian behavior, we become stiff and unnatural, especially when we blow it. People won't respect us if we take ourselves too seriously.

2. We don't take our callings seriously enough. We pastors often take the path of least resistance. We do this in the name of pastoral sensitivity, but we end up perpetuating the myth that we're wimpy, dreary lightweights when it comes to running a church.

One church I know of was having trouble keeping pastors. It

seems that earlier in its history, the senior pastor had enjoyed a long tenure, but when he retired, he kept his hand in the church's affairs. Since his "retirement," he had personally appointed many of the elders, and he had managed to run off three successors.

One of the elders noticed the pattern and, with the support of a contingent in the church, came to talk with me about becoming the church's pastor. After he described the retired pastor's pattern of interference, he said, "But I think we've finally got a majority on the board, and I think we can take him on."

"You're not looking for a pastor," I replied, "You're looking for a drill sergeant, someone mean."

"I wouldn't exactly say that," he mumbled.

"That's exactly what you're looking for. Someone who's strong enough to stand up to this man."

"Well, maybe. And we figured you're one of only two pastors we know of who could do it."

That's a sad commentary: when this man thinks of pastors, he doesn't see many strong ones.

Setting the Right Tone

I'm hardly a drill sergeant, of course. I couldn't have stayed pastor at Key Biscayne as long as I did if that were true. People need and deserve a caring pastor, and I believe they got one in me.

But people also need and deserve a leader. And that means at times you've got to be willing to "play mean," whether it's your personality or not.

Before we can expect people to take us seriously as preachers, then, they must take us seriously as pastors. Here are three ways I try to ensure that.

● *Stand up, stand up for Jesus.* Paul writes that he doesn't mind being a fool for Christ if that's what it takes to live and preach as a Christian. I'm sorry to say I'm not as courageous as Paul. But I'm convinced that the more we are willing to take public, and sometimes humbling, stands for Christ, the more our people respect what we say in the pulpit.

After graduate school at Boston University, I pastored a church in the Boston area. My own spiritual journey was slowly inching me away from the intellectual agnosticism of old liberalism to a more orthodox, Christ-centered faith. One of the men who mentored me during those days was an elderly pastor with muscular dystrophy, a short, inarticulate man who walked on crutches. He pastored a sister church close to mine, and he knew God deeply and taught me how to pray.

The local presbytery, of which we were a part, was planning to launch an inner-city ministry. Both he and I were in attendance the day the presbytery discussed the reasons for going ahead with the project. At one point in the meeting, my mentor stood up and shuffled to the front of the group.

"This inner-city ministry is a good idea," he said, "because we need people saved."

The presbytery broke out in laughter, guffawing at what seemed to most of our colleagues a presumptuous, unenlightened statement. I was one of the few who didn't snicker, but neither did I stand up for my friend. That night, I knelt down and prayed, "God, if they ever laugh at a brother or sister again, they'll laugh at two of us." I've kept that promise ever since.

I mentioned that story on one of my taped sermons, and I once received a letter from a man who was convicted about his own lack of courage. He wrote that he was riding on a commuter train in New York when a passenger stood up and started asking the people around him, in a loud, obnoxious voice, whether or not they were saved. Then he began handing out tracts.

"I started to slink down in my seat," he wrote, "ashamed of this bothersome stranger who was pushing the gospel on the other passengers. But then I remembered the story you told about not standing up for the truth. So I stood up, put my arm around him, and said to the others in the train car, 'I want you all to know that this is my brother, and I agree with everything he is saying.' "

These courageous stands don't necessarily have to be taken in view of your congregation. Don't worry. The word will get around that you stand up for what you believe. And that will mean another word will get around: that you're a pastor who has some credibility.

• *Tell people you're human.* Some of our people have no idea what goes on in a pastor's life. That means sometimes we need simply to challenge their stereotypes.

One of my associates was counseling a woman who had just admitted to an affair. She was attempting to explain why she decided to sleep with a married man when she finally blurted out, "You don't understand. You're a pastor."

Her comment so annoyed my associate, he just about jumped over his desk. "I'm not letting you get away with that," he said. "I face the same temptations you do. You can't get off the hook that easily."

He may have been a little too blunt, but that woman got the point.

An old pastor friend once told me, "Don't tell people you're a pastor, but if they find out, don't let them be surprised." I agree with that to a degree. But I don't mind when people are surprised, especially when I seem so, you know, normal! I want my people to consider me streetsmart, someone who understands the world in which they work and live.

When someone says, "Reverend, some day I'm going to take you out and show you the real world," I've been known to say, "I see more of the real world in one week than you'll see in a lifetime." I refuse to let people live in their misconceptions.

• *Don't always be nice.* I had been invited to speak at a retreat outside Atlanta. During one of the sessions, I illustrated a point by talking about my growing up with an alcoholic father. Afterwards, one of the participants tapped me on the shoulder, interrupted a conversation I was in, and said, "Steve, your father didn't love you."

"Ma'am?" I said, turning.

"Your father didn't love you," she repeated. "My husband loves our children by not drinking and by spending time with them."

I felt as if I had been slapped in the face. I blushed with anger and blurted out, "Ma'am, I wouldn't trade ten of your sober husbands for my drunk daddy!"

Most times I would have ended the conversation politely and stewed about her comment for days. I could have been more tactful. But tact isn't everything, even in the pastorate, especially if we want people to respect us.

● *Know when to say when.* In one of the churches I served, a man had given $5,000 towards the building program. He must have assumed his gift gave him the right to badger the building committee and me, for he was overbearing and negative, and he complained incessantly.

One Sunday morning, while the elders and I were gathered to pray before the service, he strode into the office and began his litany of complaints about the building project.

"Hold on a minute," I said. "You've already used up your $5,000. That's all $5,000 gets you. If you want me to listen to your complaining, you need to give more money. But that's all I'll take for now."

He was furious, naturally. And he soon left the church.

As pastors, more times than not, we need to practice patience and loving kindness with our people. But there comes a time in each pastor's ministry when he or she should no longer be patient, when patience would be a disservice to the church and to the gospel. It takes wisdom and experience to know when you can get away with such brash behavior. But it doesn't take many instances for people to get the idea that you are someone they have to reckon with.

Take the Long View

In some situations, people simply take pastors for granted. In other situations, they simply don't respect us. If that's the case, it's usually a long-term problem that needs a long-term strategy.

One church I know of had a history of running off pastors. They called one of my friends to the pastorate, and I just about died when he told me. I told him what I knew about the church: that a cantankerous majority kept the reins tight and whenever a pastor tried to challenge them, they knew how to make his life uncomfortable. I said to him, "Listen: you have to be strong when you pastor there."

About a year later, he called me and said, "You've got to help me find another church. I can't stand this anymore."

I agreed to start looking, but nothing was immediately open. In the meantime, my friend decided to take a fresh approach. He began to build a constituency in the church, to get control of the nominating committee. Gradually he put more elders of his persuasion on the board. When we talked once about this, I told him, "If you ever get a majority vote, you better run with it — and don't take any prisoners!"

I heard one sermon tape of his in which that happened. In it he said, "I had a sermon prepared this morning, but in my devotions, I was reading a passage about Moses confronting his elders. I think I've got to say some things to you. Now, I don't know whether I'm Moses and these other folks I'm about to mention are the elders, or whether they're Moses and I'm the elders, but we can't live with this anymore. We've got to get it straightened out." He went on to name people he felt were the source of the trouble.

In a few weeks, a congregational meeting was called to ask for his dismissal. But he won the vote, and he ended up staying there another seven or eight years. When he left, he left a healthy church, one with a healthy respect for its pastor.

Some people say, "Don't get mad, get even." I don't think that's Christian, but to pastors, I might say, "When people don't respect you, don't get mad, get chips." Earn the right to be strong with them by paying your pastoral dues: visit the hospital; bury the dead; perform baptisms and marriages. And along the way, slowly build a base that will allow you to preach as you need to.

Intellectual Credibility

Many people think pastors are intellectual lightweights. They don't realize the amount of study it takes to preach week after week, and they haven't a clue as to how much academic rigor we go through in seminary. I've done a couple of things to counter those types of misperceptions.

The first is an evangelistic outreach more than anything, but it had the added benefit of showing people that I was to be taken seriously at an intellectual level.

In one church, I offered what I called a "Skeptics' Forum." We printed invitations and encouraged all members to invite their atheist and agnostic friends to attend. I promised to be the only Christian there, so as not to intimidate the visitors.

The first Monday night, I let the visitors set the agenda. They told me what they wanted to talk about, what questions they had. I wrote them on a legal pad and then used that information to plan the coming weeks. Each meeting I'd take a few minutes to express the Christian view of pain or the Devil or belief in God. And then we'd have a give-and-take session for a couple of hours.

A large number of these people became Christians, and those who didn't no longer laughed at the Christian faith, nor the messenger of it.

I also teach students to use words from time to time that few in the congregation will know, to quote writers few people have read, to make a reference to things esoteric — for no other reason than to remind them that, in fact, you study a great deal to pull together sermons week after week.

Naturally, this can be overdone and usually is by young ministers, to the detriment of the clarity of their sermons. Still, when done in measure, it makes the point without getting in the way of the message. To put it crassly: they'll think you're smart, and so they'll better listen to what you say.

Preaching for Respect

There's a story about an ambassador, a short, frail man, who talked quietly whenever he was with important people. One day, somebody asked him why he always softened his voice.

"When a big man shouts, people take him seriously," he said. "But when a little man shouts, he just looks silly. So I talk quietly."

There are many ways we can effectively use the pulpit to

enhance our credibility. This ambassador understood a key one: we shouldn't violate our personalities; we should use well our natural gifts. Here are a few others.

● *Use earthy language.* Using profanity in the pulpit would turn me into a little man who shouts. Swearing only violates the integrity of the preacher and further distances him or her from the listener. But I occasionally use language that suggests stronger wording, for instance "spit," as in, "I don't give a spit!" I've also made statements like "This place has more rooms than a Chinese bordello."

I used to use "horse feathers" a lot. One of the elders came to me and said, "Steve, I wish you wouldn't do that. I know what you're doing. But every time you say "horse feathers," I think you're going to say something worse, and I just wince." So I decided to quit using the phrase.

Still, even though I occasionally offend, I look for colorful expressions that I can say naturally and that will communicate to people that I live in the same world they do.

● *No euphemisms.* By being straight with people, we also can increase the effect of our words. In stewardship sermons, for example, I might begin by saying, "You know about all the missionaries we support. Look at these staff people who minister day in and day out. You know firsthand the significance of their ministries. You know that people from our church reach out to the homeless and the AIDS babies. All this is expensive."

Then I pause and say, "Now let me get honest for a minute. If you don't support this ministry, I also don't get paid. So this subject has extreme existential importance to me!"

Though some object to my crass revelation, I know a lot of people are thinking it when I'm giving an appeal for "the ministry of the church." They know very well that if we don't make our budget, it affects my salary. So I mention it up front.

● *Be contrarian.* Making contrarian statements is a third technique to shake people up and to get them to take seriously the gospel. I often tell my students at the seminary where I teach, "If you think you shouldn't say it, you probably should."

I may be making an evangelistic appeal to my audience, and I will say, "I don't give a dink for the millions going to hell." At that moment, you see, I don't. I'll continue, "Right now, I care about you, because I know you, and I want you to respond to Christ." (I'll qualify that for some audiences, of course.)

When I've encouraged other pastors to speak like this, they frequently say, "Steve, if I said that, my people would crucify me."

My standard reply is, "No, they wouldn't. God's people are wonderful — at least 90 percent of them. If we constantly play to the 10 percent who get mad at us (and will be mad at us for eternity), we'll never communicate effectively to the other 90 percent."

One of the best compliments I've received was, "Steve, you really force people to listen. They cannot not listen." That's my goal in taking risks: gaining a hearing for the gospel of Christ.

Serious Respect

One year recently was particularly tough on me. I was cleaning up after Hurricane Andrew, and my mother had just died, when my wife, Anna, discovered a lump in her breast. I thought, *Lord, no! I don't think I can take any more. I'm not Job; I can't deal with Anna having cancer.*

We were still in North Carolina at the time, wrapping up the loose ends of my mother's estate. Anna immediately called up a friend of ours, whose husband is a doctor. She asked if she could be examined immediately.

A day or so later, the doctor examined her and assured her that everything was fine.

"I'm going to remove the lump," he said, "and then I'll send it to the pathologist. But I'm sure it's benign."

So, right there in his office, he gave her an anesthetic and surgically removed the lump. Immediately following, the doctor closed his office, and we went to lunch with him and his wife.

I can still remember the love I felt that afternoon for that doctor. I deeply respected him for his wisdom and skill, for lovingly applying his gift to me and my wife in a difficult, scary situation.

That's how I want my listeners to respond to my calling. For when they do, they will start taking seriously the message I bring, the message that can make all the difference in their difficult, scary situations.

Too much of our homiletical energy is spent reducing the gospel to a bumper sticker or acting as if it's easy to understand.

— *William Willimon*

CHAPTER FIVE
Assuming They Are Christians

In January of 1991, as the country was in the throes of the Gulf crisis with Iraq, I attended a large church for Sunday worship. During the service, the preacher gave a children's sermon.

"Boys and girls," the preacher said after the kids had scrambled to the front of the sanctuary, "what is today?"

Silence. Finally some freshly scrubbed ruffian blurted, "Sunday, January 6."

"Goooood," replied the preacher. "But today is more than that. In the church calendar, today is Epiphany. Can you say the word *Epiphany?"*

A noisy chorus of "Epiphany" reverberated throughout the sanctuary in thirty-part disharmony.

"The word means 'manifestation' or 'revelation,' " the preacher continued. "And even though you may never have heard of Epiphany, I bet everybody has heard of a favorite Epiphany story, the story of the wise men. How many of you know that story?"

Again, a commotion broke out indicating they had.

"The star revealed to these wise men, or Magi, that Jesus was the long-awaited Messiah. Matthew begins his Gospel by saying these Magi were the first to come to see the baby Jesus. The Epiphany question for today is, 'Where did the Magi come from?' "

"From the East?" a child said.

"Gooood," the preacher replied. "They came from the East. But where did they come from in the East? Yes, Persia. Persia is the biblical way of talking about the East. Persia was east of the Holy Land. Now where is Persia on this map, boys and girls?"

"Uh, Iran?"

"Yes, Iran. But that's not all of Persia," replied the persistent pastor.

"Iraq?"

"Gooood, Iraq," he said. "And Baghdad was sort of the capital of Persia. So today, Epiphany, is the day the church gets together and says, 'Thank you, God, for sending us three Iraqis, who saw the baby Jesus before us Bible-believing people did.' Now you can all go back to your seats to be with your parents."

As the children filed back to their seats, the congregation fumbled for their seat belts. A simple children's story had broadsided the entire congregation with the transnational claim of the gospel, throwing their American experience into a larger picture, where God is the Lord of all.

Too often we preachers, in our attempt to be relevant, do the exact opposite of this presumptuous preacher: we begin with the world of the listener instead of the peculiar truths of Scripture —

what I call experienced-based or inductive preaching. We begin our Sunday preparation by saying essentially, "What is my audience interested in?" We assume our task is simply to awaken in our audience those basic human impulses we arrive on the scene with.

One of my friends, a biblical scholar, mentioned to me that too many sermons he hears address no one in particular, much less those who are baptized. His comment prodded me to think about what preaching to the baptized might mean, and I've come to at least three conclusions.

Translation Problems

To preach to the baptized means, first, that we must do business with this text, the Scripture, before we can go to other texts. I'm not free to put the gospel through a psychological or a political sieve. I'm not free to translate the gospel into, say, the reigning philosophy of the day.

How many of us have started a Sunday morning sermon by saying to our audience something like, "Have you ever been depressed? Well, the Bible speaks to our depression, and if you'll turn to this morning's text, we'll discover what God's Word has to say about our problem."

The week leading up to that week's sermon, we probably ransacked our brains to find a current need of our congregation, and then we rummaged around the Bible to find something helpful to speak to that aspect of human experience.

This is the problem with much of modern preaching: it starts with gut-level human experience, namely our therapeutically saturated culture, and then attempts to work backward to the Bible.

I returned to pastoral ministry after having taught for several years, and I experienced this pull. I was surprised, for instance, by how much of a pastor's time is spent with depressed people. There seems to be an epidemic of depression.

Not long after returning to parish life, I received a phone call from a depressed woman. "Pastor, can you come over this morning? I'm not doing very well today. I'm feeling sort of down and blue. Are you busy?"

I told her I'd drop by that afternoon and pray with her in the hopes I might encourage her. Then I returned to the Jeremiah commentary I was reading, which would, it turned out, help me a great deal. The passage under discussion concerned Jeremiah's calling Israel to grieve for their sins. Only by grieving, said the commentator, could Israel begin to let go of the mundane status quo and gain a fresh vision from God of what their world could be about. The vision would come only after the tears.

By the time I drove to that woman's house, I had a different mode of pastoral care to offer her. Instead of addressing her depression with therapeutic answers, I said, "Forgive me. I've been treating you as if you were sick or something. I know you're depressed, but that's good. A lot of people think this town is a great place to live. But you're an intelligent, creative person, and you realize intuitively there's a sickness here — people are too materialistic and too self-occupied. You're depressed about it. You are waiting in your $300,000 home —"

"$350,000," she interrupted.

"— in your $350,000 home, waiting for your husband to come home on Friday and make your day. I know your husband — he's not capable of that! No human being is. The good news is that you know you need more, and you're in grief. That's a good start. We can work with this. We couldn't work with you when you were happy."

Who taught me to name what is happening to her as "depression"? We did not get that word from the Bible. I cannot make any connection between the "Why are you cast down, O my soul?" of the Psalms and what we call psychological depression. I believe she was not experiencing depression but a form of spiritual despair.

I'm called to teach a new language, a different way of naming the pain, and everything hinges on how we name that pain. We should name that pain in the way the Bible names it.

George Lindbeck of Yale University says Americans have been conditioned to think of religion as an innate, inborn trait, and that different religions, such as Buddhism and Christianity, are different ways of expressing this innate, pan-human phenomenon.

But the way each religion speaks about its deity and doctrines, says Lindbeck, is much different, so much so that one quickly discovers that Christians and Buddhists, for example, speak of two very different gods. The way they describe their allegiances indicates a much different relationship and hence two distinct deities.

In the same way, theology of the Bible and that of our therapeutically drenched culture are not easily transferable. Too much is lost in the translation. The preacher's first question, then, is not "What are my listeners' concerns?" but "What does the gospel say?"

Speaking the Language

One of the best compliments I've received was after an Easter sermon in which I'd said, "Easter is not about the return of the robin in spring or blooming crocuses or butterflies coming out of their cocoons or any of that pagan drivel. It's about a body that somehow got loose. The gospel accounts strain to describe what happened, but don't make any mistake about it, they're trying to describe something unearthly: death working backward.

"So I can't talk about 'the eternal rebirth of hope' or 'Jesus living on in our hearts.' We're talking about a dead Jew, crucified, who came back to harass us. And it scares the heck out of us!"

A student came up to me and said, "Thank you for helping me articulate what I don't believe." By explaining what the Resurrection truly means to Christians, I had confirmed his unbelief. At least he took my preaching, and the gospel, seriously.

That's the second characteristic of preaching to the baptized — giving biblical definitions priority.

In Acts 17, Paul speaks to the people of Athens, bringing the gospel into collision with their ideas. He calls them religious, but what they don't know is that it's not really a compliment. Then he makes a joke about their never seeing an idol they couldn't worship. Before long he's telling them about the God they don't know and bringing up the Resurrection, for which he gets the typical Gentile response of mockery and polite, philosophical interest.

I see here an invitation and a warning to preachers who want to contextualize the gospel. The invitation is to start where the people are, but the warning is to recognize our limited ability to adapt the gospel. Eventually the gospel is about something for which there is no precedent — the Resurrection — and we can only testify to it. The truth claims of Christianity are not easily validated externally. They're a matter of faith.

By giving biblical definitions priority in our messages, we're communicating that to be in the church means to enter a new epistemology. *Epistemology* is simply a fancy word for the questions "How do we know what we know? How do we get our information about the world?" The baptized derive their epistemology from the Bible. Christian speech — *baptism, redemption, sin* — is not psychological speech — *depression, codependency, addiction*. In fact, the Bible claims that we cannot even fully hear what the preacher is saying unless we're born again.

To understand fully Christian speech requires a radical transformation, a detoxification, a born-again conversion — however you wish to speak of it. Someone who comes on board with Jesus is someone who's empowered, washed, cleaned up, dead and buried, raised, adopted — the images are all baptismal.

French isn't learned by reading a French novel in an English translation. You have to take French; you have to learn the verbs. There's no way around the pain of learning the declensions and conjugations. The baptized, then, will need to be steeped in the language of their conversion. This is the job of the Christian preacher.

Making an Assault

Being baptized means to stand under the Word, to be willing to be transformed. If I join the Rotary Club, I'm handed a lapel pin, a membership card, and given a handshake. But if I join the church, the pastor throws me into the water, half-drowns me, brings me up, and then calls me "Brother." Baptism, which is nothing short of strange, is supposed to create a new people who look at the world quite differently than before.

Third, then, to preach to the baptized means to allow Scripture to transform people. The Bible doesn't want to speak to the modern world; the Bible wants to create a world that would not have been there without the speaking of the Bible.

We pastors have spent far too much of our homiletical energy reducing the gospel to a bumper sticker or acting as if it's easy to understand. Instead, we ought to remind people how very difficult it is. In fact, we're called to assault the prevailing norms with the gospel. And in the process of hearing the gospel, God's new community begins to take shape.

I sometimes say, "All right, folks, just for this morning, let's all trust this Word from God more than we trust our feelings or our experience. The gospel isn't trying to explore your experience but to engender a new experience. It's trying to take you someplace you've never been. Let's see where that takes us."

In one sense, Sunday morning is a game with one important rule: this ancient, confusing, assaulting, and wonderfully challenging book — the Bible — knows more about truth than we do. After I've preached a sermon, I've had people say to me, "That's the strangest thing I've ever heard. I've never heard anything like that before."

The pastoral-homiletical response should be "Hey, don't complain to me. I'm not the one who called you forth to be baptized. It's out of my hands. You're the one who wanted to be baptized. These aren't my stories. This stuff is not original with me. But it is for the baptized.

"To me you look like an average American, but since you're baptized, evidently Jesus has a great deal of faith in your ability to hear this sort of stuff."

If someone complains, "Well now, how am I supposed to run a hardware store on the basis of that?" we should say, "I don't know. That's not my problem. My baptismal priority, bestowed to me through ordination, is to explain the gospel to you. Your baptismal priority is to live those truths in the world as Jesus' priests."

During the Gulf crisis, my associate one Sunday morning prayed for the Iraqi soldiers and their families. A woman complained about the prayer.

"The prayer?" I asked, incredulous.

"Yes," she said. "I think it's just so important for us to stand behind the president."

"Let's get this straight," I said. "We're Christians. Jesus has commanded us to pray for our enemies. I know it doesn't come easy, so that's why we work at it for an hour or so on Sunday morning. We hope eventually we'll get good at it. But this is non-negotiable; that's the way Christians are commanded to pray."

Our people arrive to be baptized with all of their advanced degrees and sophistication. But that needs to get stripped off, washed away. Martin Luther said that we never get too old or too smart to die. Every day we're asked to die, take up our crosses, and follow Jesus. Christians, says Luther, are those who jump out of bed every morning and say, "Good morning, Jesus. Continue to put me to death."

Our preaching must enable our listeners to die, continuing that baptismal work done at their baptism, so new creatures might continue to be raised, week after week.

The Imperial Gospel

A good question to ask at the end of any sermon is "Would they have killed Jesus for this?" Not all of my sermons stand up to that question; the death of Jesus would seem incomprehensible over some of the bland stuff I've preached. People would be more apt to make Jesus president of a university or a speaker for a weekend conference. If I don't watch myself, I can reduce Christianity to merely being a good person, someone who is gung ho for society.

People had good reason to crucify Jesus. They recognized in him a threat to the world as it was constituted, and he continues to be a threat. I love Jesus for being outrageous. I want my preaching to say, "What did you think we were talking about here — Santa Claus? Hey, this is *God* we're talking about, a real God, not some projection of your ego."

One Duke student was telling me he was losing his faith. I asked him, "What is the faith you're losing?"

"I don't believe in the Virgin Birth anymore."

"So what? You're a sexually active college student," I replied. "You don't believe in virginity, period! You're 19 years old; there's a lot you don't know yet. Why don't you just wait awhile to see how your doctrine works out."

Then he asked a good question: "Why do you have to swallow stuff like this to be a Christian?"

"Well," I said, "when we get you to believe these easy things, then you're ready for the tougher demands of Christianity: how to live this faith, turning the other cheek, letting go of your Duke degree and all the power it's going to give you. We start with the Virgin Birth because it's simple. Then we'll work you up to the tough stuff, like making Jesus Lord of your life."

Sidestepping the intrusive, imperialistic claims of the gospel is not an option if we intend to preach to the baptized. We are not free to exchange gospel foolishness for the wisdom of this world. As Christian preachers preaching to Christian people, we're obligated to preach Christian truths.

A sermon full of generalities hits no one in particular.
— Haddon Robinson

CHAPTER SIX

All Things
to All People

While Grace Chapel in Lexington, Massachusetts, was without a pastor for over a year, I preached there often. The church is remarkably diverse, having Harvard professors and high school dropouts, doctors and lawyers as well as house cleaners, political activists and those who don't even read the newspaper, people with multimillion dollar investment portfolios and minimum-wage workers. In addition, members are of many races and colors.

I stood before such diversity each week amazed at the responsibility I had to reach them all. As I prepared my sermons, I stewed over how my sermon could reach the entire cross section.

As preachers, our task can be expressed simply: to become all things to all people. To actually do it is a formidable task.

Sobering Demands

When we fail to speak to the entire cross section in our churches, it is often because we act like the doctor who has only two answers; as long as a patient asks the right two questions, the doctor can help. Or we resemble the doctor who only knows how to set a broken arm: if a patient complains of a bellyache, the doctor breaks her arm so he can set it.

Reaching broader audiences makes sobering demands on us.

● *Sacrifice what comes natural.* When Paul said, "I have become all things to all men, that I may by all means save some" (1 Cor. 9:22), he wasn't talking just about evangelism. He was also talking about helping converts grow. "To the weak," to believers who had weak consciences, he became weak; he restricted his freedom for their sakes.

Speaking to a broader audience requires a sacrifice from us. We give up our freedom to use certain kinds of humor, to call minority groups by names that make sense to us, to illustrate only from books and movies we find interesting, to speak only to people with our education and level of Christian commitment. Sometimes such sacrifice feels constricting.

A pastor who objects strongly to the women's movement, for example, might take a passing shot at its leaders and activities. By doing so, though, he risks needlessly alienating many women in the congregation.

Sacrificing what comes most naturally to us, though, is what gives us a platform to speak. Just as a legalistic Jew wouldn't regard Paul as credible if Paul ignored the law, so many women, for example, won't regard a preacher as credible if he shows zero sensitivity to their issues.

Why go to all this trouble? First, because it is right, and then because it is wise. Because the people we are most likely to offend are those on the edge, those cautiously considering the gospel or deeper commitment but who are skittish, easily chased away by one offensive move from pastors. Those already secure in the fold will probably stick by us in spite of our blunders. The new people we're trying to reach are as easily spooked as wild turkeys.

A young couple moved into a Chicago suburb and attended one church for several months. The church helped them through the husband's unemployment. Several times the pastor met with the man, who had advanced degrees in ecology and was interested in deeper involvement in the church.

Then he and his wife abruptly stopped coming. The pastor repeatedly tried to contact them, and finally after several months, he was able to take the man out for lunch. He asked him why they had not come to church in such a long time.

"In several of your sermons," the man replied, "you made comments that belittled science. If that is the way you feel, I don't think we're on the same wavelength."

The pastor remembered the remarks, which were either passing comments or rhetorical flourishes contrasting the power of Christ and the weakness of humankind. But the consequence was not passing: a man who showed promise of moving into deeper discipleship had been diverted.

• *Reach people where they are.* The Bible is nothing if not a casebook of how to bring truth to people where they are. In the Gospels we see that Christ never dealt with two people the same way. He told the curious Pharisee that he needed to be born again, the woman at the well that she needed living water. He brought good news to each individual, but he did so at the person's point of contact.

The New Testament epistles differ from each other because they brought the same basic theology to bear on diverse problems. In 1 Corinthians Paul defended the doctrine of the Resurrection against those who doubted it; in 1 Thessalonians Paul brought that same truth to believers who were worried about what would happen to those who had already died in Christ.

From beginning to end, we see God adjusting the message to the audience without sacrificing the truth — same theology, different questions. Truth is never more powerfully experienced than when it speaks to someone's personal situation.

Target-group Preaching

When we try not to exclude listeners, we are tempted to preach in generalities. For example, if I say, "Irritation bothers us all," I'm speaking to no one in particular. A sermon full of generalities hits no one in particular.

We do better to focus specifically on two or three types of people in a message (changing who those two or three groups are each week). The surprising thing is that the more directed and personal a message, the more universal it becomes.

I might illustrate a sermon on conflict by saying, "You live with your roommate, and your roommate has some irritating habits — like not cleaning the dishes right after the meal. Or you're married, and your husband comes home and plops himself in front of the TV without any regard for what your day has been like." Although I don't address the situations of many listeners directly, they can identify with these common experiences and the feelings they elicit.

A few times a year, I may preach an entire sermon to one particular group in the church.

"This morning I want to talk to young men or women in business, twenty-eight years of age, with your eyes on a long and successful career. Jesus is talking about someone like you in this text. I'm not talking this morning to the retired person. I'm looking at those on their way up the ladder."

Or, "This morning I want to talk only to the teenagers. Some of you adults enjoy a short winter's nap on Sunday morning anyway, but this morning I give you permission to do so. Today I want to talk to young people in junior and senior high. You are an important part of this church, and I'd appreciate it if you would listen."

All the application in that sermon would be for young people, but only a rare adult would tune out. In fact, information overheard can be more influential than information received directly. When you come right out and tell the congregation you're addressing a limited group, ironically, it galvanizes everyone's interest. Specificity is far more effective than giving general principles and saying, "May the Holy Spirit help each of us to apply this to our lives."

In order to anticipate in some measure what different members of an audience may be going through, I use a suggestion given to me by a good friend, Don Sunukjian. I prepare my sermons using a life-situation grid. Across the top of the grid, I label columns for men, women, singles, married, divorced, those living together. On the side of the grid, I have a row that includes categories for different age groups (youth, young adult, middle-age, elderly), professional groups (the unemployed, the self-employed, workers, and management), levels of faith (committed Christians, doubters, cynics, and atheists), the sick and the healthy, to name a few. I develop my grid based on the congregation and community I am preaching to.

After I've researched my text and developed my ideas, I wander around in the grid looking for two to four intersections where the message will be especially relevant. For instance, in one sermon on money, based on the parable of the shrewd branch manager in Luke 16, I went through my grid and thought of a widow in the congregation whose husband had been the president of a major corporation and had left her a large amount of money. She once had said to me, "What a curse it is to have a lot of money and take God seriously." Since I knew others in the congregation had significant incomes, I thought specifically about how someone with more money than they know what to do with would hear and feel about this passage.

But hers wasn't the only situation I was concerned with. A second intersection on the grid I explored was the working poor.

A third group of special concern was those visiting the church for the first time who would say afterward, "All pastors do is preach about money."

For those with no discretionary funds, I talked about how Christ focuses on the attitude of our hearts, not on the amount we give. And for church visitors, I included some humor and spoke directly to the objection.

I regularly update my grid with new insights I gain about people.

For instance, after one service a woman told me how she and

several other African-Americans had taken out an ad in the *New York Times* to explain their resentment of homosexual activists drawing on the black experience to describe their experience. "They identified themselves as a minority," she told me. "We're both minorities, but that's the only thing we have in common. They don't know what we've gone through. They don't know the pain of being black."

She helped me understand what a disadvantaged minority feels, and someday I'm sure I'll include in a sermon how God can help those who feel the pain of being black in America.

How can we gain an appreciation for lives unlike our own, from cleaning ladies to investment bankers? The same way novelists do: by listening and observing. Pay attention to the people you counsel, the conversations around you in restaurants and stores, to characters in novels and movies, to common people interviewed on the news. Note how these people state their concerns, note their specific phrasing, their feelings, their issues. Get an ear for dialogue.

I know one pastor who holds a focus group each Thursday before he preaches. He eats lunch with several people from diverse backgrounds, tells them the ideas in his sermon, and asks them how they hear these ideas. They often raise issues that had never occurred to him.

In addition to applying a message broadly, I try to illustrate broadly. I am tempted to draw many of my illustrations from sports, which may not appeal to the majority of women (who, significantly, comprise more than half of most congregations). I intentionally try to include illustrations that women identify with, stories focused on relationships, drawn from the worlds of home and family or what they experience in the workplace.

As I watch TV I look for illustrations. My own tendency is to draw from what I read, but most people in a congregation do not read the materials I read. They live in a different sphere from mine, and I try to honor that in my sermons.

The Most Common Ground

Pastors preach each week to diverse congregations, but their listeners have a great deal in common. Every person in the pew has these desires:

— They want to meet God or run away from him.

— They want to learn something.

— They want to laugh.

— They want to feel significant.

— They want to be motivated, in a positive way, to do better.

— They want a pastor to understand their pain and the difficulty they have doing what's right, without letting them off the hook.

One of the most important tools for addressing these universal concerns is through illustrations. People identify with people more than ideas. They gossip about people, not principles. Though they are grounded in specifics, good stories transcend individual experiences so that people from a variety of situations can gain something from them. When hearing a story, listeners tell the story to themselves, inserting their own experiences and images.

An older woman once said to me, "Sometimes the Christian life is like washing sheets." She described how she washed sheets by hand in a large washing bucket, how she would push one part of the sheet under water and air bubbles would move to another part of the sheet and float that section above water.

"I push it down here, it comes up there," she said. "I can never keep the whole sheet under water."

As she described the scene, her story became my story. My mind jumped back a half century to my boyhood. I recalled my mother washing clothes in a tub and having the same problem.

Furthermore, in stories, listeners put themselves into the scene, becoming participants of the story.

I heard Gordon MacDonald, preaching about John the Baptist, tell this story: Several management types were at the River Jordan as the crowds came to John, and they decided they needed to get things organized. So they set up tables and begin to give tags to those coming for repentance. On the tag is written the person's name and chief sin. Bob walks up to the table. The organizers write his name on the tag and then ask, "What's your most awful sin, Bob?"

"I stole some money from my boss."

The person at the table takes a marker and writes in bold letters, EMBEZZLER, and slaps it on Bob's chest.

The next person comes forward. "Name?"

"Mary."

"Mary, what's your most awful sin?"

"I gossiped about some people. It wasn't very much, but I didn't like these people."

The organizers write, MARY — SLANDERER, and slap it on her.

A man walks up to the table. "Name?"

"George."

"George, what's your most awful sin?"

"I've thought about how nice it would be to have my neighbor's Corvette."

GEORGE — COVETER.

Another man approaches the table. "What's your name?" he is asked.

"Gordon."

"What's your sin?"

"I've had an affair."

The organizer writes, GORDON — ADULTERER, and slaps the sticker on his chest.

Soon Christ comes to be baptized. He walks down the line of those waiting to be baptized and asks them for their sin tags. One by one, he takes those tags off the people and sticks them on his own body. He goes to John, and as he is baptized, the river washes away the ink from each name tag he bears.

As Gordon told that story, everyone in the congregation mentally wrote their own sin and slapped it on their own chests.

To come up with images and stories, I sometimes write idea networks on a sheet of paper. If I'm talking about home, for example, I'll write the word *home* in the center of a sheet of paper, circle the word, and then surround it with any associations that come to my mind: "home sweet home," "welcome home," "it's good to have you home again," "home on the range," "going home for Christmas," "stole home."

These associations will in turn inspire other associations and memories, some personal, some cultural. What I'm doing is digging into the phrases and images our culture associates with home. Somewhere from that page I'll come up with one or more images or stories with larger appeal.

On Their Side

I do everything I can to show people I respect them and I'm on their side. It's another way I try to be all things to all people.

For instance, in my preaching I cultivate a conversational tone. Many people in our culture resent an authoritarian, lecturing manner. That style is what moderns mean when they use *preaching* in a pejorative sense ("Don't preach at me!"). They consider it patronizing and narrow-minded.

I also show empathy. When I quote from Malachi, "God hates divorce," I know there are divorced people sitting in the congregation who may begin to feel that God and Haddon Robinson hate them. So I'll follow up that verse with, "Those of you who are divorced know that better than anyone. You understand why God hates divorce. Not because he hates divorced people but because of what divorce does to people. You have the scars. Your children have the scars. You can testify to what it does. God hates divorce because he loves you."

I've found if listeners know you love and identify with them, they will let you say strong things. Most people are just asking that you be aware of them and not write them off.

I'm careful about terms. Even though you're sure you don't have a bias, a listener may think you do if your phrasing offends them.

I try to use gender-inclusive language. If I'm telling a story about a doctor, I might say, "A surgeon stands in the operating room. As she takes the scalpel in her hand. . . ." I intentionally use *she* over *he* in strategic spots to signal that I know women can be surgeons and lawyers and presidents.

I employ terms like *spokesperson* instead of *spokesman*. I say "he or she" instead of always saying *he*; or I use *he* sometimes and *she* other times. Such uses don't have to be split fifty/fifty; even a few female pronouns in a sermon make a difference. Here's a radical experiment: try using *she* all through a sermon except when you must use the masculine pronoun. You will get a sense of how much of our preaching has a male flavor.

I call minority groups what they want to be called. If someone's name is Charles, and he doesn't like being called Charlie or Chuck, I'm obligated to call him Charles. I used to say *Negroes*, then *Blacks*. I used the term *Afro-American* in a recent sermon, and afterward a woman kindly corrected me, "It's African-American."

Of course, no matter how hard we try, we're still going to offend people.

Sometimes we need to apologize from the pulpit. "In last week's sermon, my humor was in bad taste. I described overweight people with a term that was hurtful. I'm sorry. I sometimes say things I don't mean, and you're gracious enough to tell me about it. Bear with me."

While preaching at Grace Chapel, I received at least a letter a week reacting to my sermons. When someone writes me, I always write back.

Some people send thoughtful letters, and I owe them a thoughtful response. Sometimes they're dead right; they catch me in a prejudice. I have to admit that.

Sometimes you get letters in which people are vitriolic through no fault of yours. The best you can do is say, "Thank you for writing. I'm sorry I offended you. I wanted to communicate a great truth of Scripture and failed to get that across to you. I'm sorry."

Hazardous Land Mines

If we focus too hard on not offending, or if we read too many letters from the offended, we can become paralyzed. We start qualifying every sentence. We end up with weasel sermons that are defensive, cautious, and spineless.

Yes, at Christmas we need to acknowledge that for some people it's the most depressing time of the year, but we can't let that rob the season's joy from the congregation. Yes, on Mother's Day childless women feel extra pain, and we can acknowledge that, but everyone has a mother to honor, and we shouldn't squelch the church's honoring of them. Although I'm aware of the land mines, I assume my listeners are usually forbearing and understanding. If I make a mistake, I can apologize. I've found the majority give a pastor the benefit of the doubt.

I try not to get uptight, defensive, or hostile in the pulpit, for that only provokes people to be more easily offended. Saying, "You shouldn't be so sensitive," or "I get so sick of all this politically correct language," does no one — you or your people — any good.

And there are those times when a pastor must preach truth at the expense of some sensitivities, yet we must do so with a burden in our hearts, not chips on our shoulders. There is no greater courage required of pastors than to preach what may cost them their pulpits.

There will always be a healthy discomfort as we try to be all things to all people. It's biblical, but it demands we walk a fine line. We want to be as appealing as possible but not at the cost of compromising the message. When we walk that line well, though, we experience something unequaled: a variety of people with a variety of concerns from a variety of settings all attentively listening to the good news.

People fail in their obedience not because we make the gospel too good but because we don't make it good enough.

— Steve Brown

CHAPTER SEVEN

Handling the Hard Side of the Gospel

Years ago I preached a strong sermon on the subject of divorce. I held no punches, and to drive home my passion about the sinfulness of divorce, I said, "I, for one, will never get a divorce!"

Later that week, the wife of the chairman of the church board came to my office. Both she and her husband had been previously divorced, though in each case, I learned in retrospect, they had biblical justification. She was hurt and angry about the sermon, "You shouldn't be so judgmental," she said.

I didn't understand what she was talking about, and I wasn't about to "wimp out" on what I thought were clear biblical principles. So I defended myself.

What she said stuck with me, however. Years later, I looked back on that message and realized she was essentially right. Not that the teaching was wrong, but my attitude was. When I said, "I will never get a divorce!" I was acting elitist, looking down my nose at people, and they deserved better than that.

"The gospel faithfully preached meddles with everything else on earth," said Henry Ward Beecher. Especially when we preach the hard truths of the gospel, we know what Beecher means. The gospel invades every nook and cranny of hearers' lives: their sexuality, thoughts, dreams, bank accounts, secret sins, goals, priorities, motivations, family, work.

We want to "meddle" but without self-righteousness. We want to build up the congregation, not condemn it. We want to speak the truth but do so in love.

So how do we do that?

Grace First and Last

In an Episcopal church, an older woman came forward for Communion and knelt alongside others. She had been troubled about her own sinfulness, and as she knelt there, she felt increasingly weighed down with guilt. When the priest approached with the bread, she was overwhelmed with her unworthiness to receive the body of Christ, so she began to back away from the Communion rail. The priest, however, quickly placed the wafer in front of her lips and said, "Take it, woman. It's for sinners. It's for you."

This is my fundamental approach not only to Communion but also to preaching: it is for sinners, and its basis is pure grace. This is especially true when it comes to preaching the hard side of the gospel. Unless I'm clear on the priority of radical grace, I will never be able to preach the hard side of the gospel effectively.

I once knew a preacher who had a reputation for prophetic preaching. He preached against false doctrine, against sin, against this and that, and he did so with great poise. He wielded the sword well, and everybody told him he was wonderful.

He was offered a church once, and he mentioned to me in a rather arrogant way that one of the elders of this church smoked cigars. He had called to ask me what I thought of him taking the church. We finally got around to the point.

"Do you want me to tell you the truth, or do you want me to say nice things to you?" I asked.

"Just tell me the truth."

"I don't think you should take that church because I don't think you can love those people. Until you sin big enough and live long enough, you will not be the pastor they need. Your problem is everybody tells you you're a wonderful preacher. When you make people feel guilty, they compliment you so you won't think they've committed that sin. If you go to that church, you'll think you're the best thing since Spurgeon, but people will feel condemned and guilty all the time."

What this preacher didn't realize, and what a great many pastors don't realize, is that people walk into the church already feeling guilty and condemned. I don't have to tell a man who is sleeping with his secretary that he's doing wrong. He knows he's doing wrong, especially if he's a believer. In fact, in twenty-eight years as a pastor, I've never met a Christian who didn't want to be better.

Furthermore, as C.S. Lewis eloquently argued in *Mere Christianity*, unbelievers also have an internal moral compass. They know instinctively when they've done wrong, and if they bother to show up in church some Sunday, it's not because they think everything is just fine!

So I don't have to convict people of their sin; the Holy Spirit is already at work in their lives. But I do have to let people know what they don't know: that grace is real, that it is unmerited, that it is unconditional. No ifs, ands, or buts.

Martin Lloyd Jones, the great British preacher, once said that if you're not nearly antinomian, you're not a Christian. He was preaching out of the Book of Romans at the time. He said if you don't see grace as the first and last word of the Christian life, if you're not a borderline heretic about grace, you've not understood the radical message of the New Testament.

This radical grace, of course, is frightening because it seems to open the door to sin. It's subject to so much misunderstanding, you don't write about it without a great deal of qualification. My book *When Being Good Isn't Good Enough* is really an argument for radical grace, and I think I would have been brought up on charges of antinomianism had I not quoted Calvin, Martin Lloyd Jones, and Spurgeon a few times!

We're so worried about people acting right that when it comes time to talk about acting right, we end up talking about just that. We inadvertently preach sermons that, if the name of Jesus were removed, could be preached by any Pharisee. We sound like common moralists.

As frightening as it is, though, we're not going to make much progress in preaching the hard side of the gospel, and not much progress with people's sanctification, until we preach from grace to grace.

An attractive and successful-looking woman came to me for counseling once. After a few minutes, she told me her dark secret: before marrying she had worked for years as a prostitute in Las Vegas. Though she had been a devoted follower of Christ for years, she was still weighed down with guilt.

In another instance, I spoke with a couple who later became leaders in the Key Biscayne church. But their marriage of twenty-five years had started on a perverse note, and they were deeply troubled by it: the man and his best friend had each divorced his own wife and married his friend's wife. In essence, they had swapped spouses. It not only affected the man and his wife but their children, as well. When they finally opened up about this, they just sat there and cried.

In both these examples, these people didn't need a moralistic chastisement — they had been living faithful lives together for years. What they needed was to understand and experience grace.

These are precisely the type of people I want to reach and raise up in Christ — sinners. Unless grace is the foundation of all they hear, they are not going far in their Christian lives. I remind myself constantly that people fail in their obedience not because we make the gospel too good but because we don't make it good enough. Only when they see how utterly amazing and lovely is the grace of God are people thankful enough, motivated enough to give their hearts, souls, and minds to God. When grace is the foundation, speaking the hard side of the gospel becomes a piece of cake. Well, almost.

Know Thyself

When I attended classes at Boston University, a student working on his doctoral thesis at Harvard interviewed me for several hours. He wanted to find out why people went into full-time Christian service. After interviewing dozens of ministers, he concluded that most are motivated by guilt.

That's bad for them and for the people in their churches. Guilt-laden pastors make other people feel guilty. Forgiven pastors, people who live under grace, set other people free.

The first thing pastors have to do before they preach a hard word to their congregations is to take a hard look at themselves, at their own motivations.

Latent guilt is certainly one key issue to address. We have to be aware of what I call the Scarlet Letter syndrome. We preach out of our own sense of unworthiness. If we struggle with pornography, that's the problem we attack most often and most fiercely. Or it may be greed or pride or envy. But if we're motivated to preach the hard news because of our guilt, we're not going to produce much lasting fruit.

Another issue is anger. We were in the middle of a huge building program at Key Biscayne Presbyterian Church when I found myself angry with a key member. He had written letters to everybody in the congregation, letters in which he criticized me and the building committee. The building committee held thirteen meetings around the city to explain the program to the congregation, and this man attended every one! After so many attacks, the chairman's wife came to me in tears: "I'm not doing this any more!"

My anger gradually rose, to the point that I began preaching at this man and his party in my sermons. One time while preaching, I walked over and stood on the side of the church in which he sat. I stepped as close to him as I could and practically talked to him. I don't know if anybody else knew what was going on, but he knew. I'm not proud of that. It was totally inappropriate.

The more we are in touch with our emotions, then, the less we'll make such blunders in the hard sermons.

There are many ways to get in touch with that part of ourselves.

Certainly prayer is the place to start. Long ago, a basic prayer of mine became, "Lord, show me myself." Often in my morning prayers, I begin with personal confession, asking God to search me: "Lord don't let me off the hook. I don't want to play the game of denial. Show me what's really going on inside me." Much to my discomfort, God shows me!

I've found reading helps. Larry Crabb's *Inside Out* (NavPress, 1988) and Sidney Jourard's *Transparent Self: Self-Disclosure and Well-Being* (Van Nos Reinhold, 1971) have been two books that have helped me look at my motivations honestly.

The best way, though, is to find a fellow believer who can be a "soul companion." It's something you have to pray about, for this is not the type of thing you can do with anybody. But I, for one, have found it immensely helpful to have a friend before whom I can take off my professional mask. We tell each other what we're really thinking and feeling, and what we see going on in the other.

Through this process, I've discovered many hidden motives and sins, and that has made me a more sensitive preacher against sin. It's hard to be self-righteously judgmental when you know your own sin all too well.

More importantly, it's put me more in touch with the wonder of grace. Evangelist and professor Michael Green once held a wine-tasting party as a way to reach out to non-believers. As people sipped Chablis, Christians tried to steer conversations to spiritual matters. One woman, a professor, unfortunately got a little tipsy in the process. She leaned over to Michael at one point and said, "You know, I don't believe any of this."

He replied, "Yeah, I know." Then he added, "But wouldn't

you like to?" Tears began welling up in her eyes.

Sometimes even preachers find the utter graciousness of God too good to be true. But that's what we discover again and again as we explore our selves. And when that grace is experienced anew, we're almost ready to preach the hard news.

How Much Can They Bear?

George Buttrick, a great preacher of the last generation, said you can't preach some things until you've been with a congregation three years. Others things you can't say until you've been there five years. For other things still, it's fifteen years.

That's another way of saying we've got to know how much of a load our relationships with congregations can bear. And the key to that is living with them in a spirit of the gospel we long to proclaim so forcefully.

One evening my elder board did something I found particularly galling. They turned down an associate staff member's request for help in buying a home. Then after the vote, they all got in their cars and left. I was in my study at the time, and they sent the youngest elder to tell me what had happened. I was so angry, I scared the young man, who knocked over a lamp as he backed out of the room.

I ran out to the parking lot, but everyone was gone. So I drove to the home of the nearest elder and knocked on his door. He was already in his pajamas. He came out on the front porch, and I started yelling at him.

"Now, calm down, Steve. Calm down," he finally said, "Are you going to talk to the other elders this way?"

"You better believe it!" I said.

"Look, you yelled at me a lot, and I understand. But some of those guys are new to the board. You be careful."

I went to another board member's home and paced his living room floor, ranting and raving about the injustice to this associate.

The next morning, he called me and said, "How are you doing, slugger?"

"Oh, all right."

"I want you to know that my dog was hiding under the couch last night."

I eventually apologized for my outburst, and the board graciously forgave me.

The point is we had established good relationships on that board. They knew I did foolish things like that. They also knew that more than anything I wanted to live faithfully for Christ. We had apologized to one another more than a few times.

Only in that atmosphere of love and forgiveness could I get away with preaching the hard news of the Bible.

Know Thy People

Nothing shocks me anymore. No one, whether churched or unchurched, can confess a sin that raises my eyebrows. We've all heard, "Pastor, you don't know what it's like in the real world." We know that's baloney. I see more of the "real world" in a week than others see in a year. I've cleaned up after more suicides and buried more babies and listened to more tortured confessions than I care to remember. It's not hard to believe in pervasive depravity.

So when I preach, I assume the worst in people. First, it's an empirical fact that people are capable of the worst. Second, I've come to see that, paradoxically, people make better progress along the sanctification road when I assume they are miserable sinners.

Here are some specific ways I do that.

● *Let the Bible do the talking.* Just because grace is first and last doesn't mean we don't frankly deal with sin. We're not offering The Ten Suggestions, after all. But I try to make sure people know that it's not my word that indicts us but the Bible's.

I've sometimes started sermons on divorce like this: "I realize that half of you have been divorced. In some ways, I wish I could skip this passage, but I can't do that, because we're about God here. And this is what God says."

And I'll introduce the sin in a non-threatening way, as in

Isaiah, when God says, "Let us reason together . . ."

I might say, "People, come on now. You don't want God ticked off — that's why you've chosen to follow him. But this is what he says: you can't come to worship with a prideful attitude. It's just not going to work. As God says . . ."

• *Place yourself in their pews.* People are not going to let me be a messenger of the hard word unless I let them know that I stand under that same word myself. So I often acknowledge my own shortcomings from the pulpit.

For instance, I have often admitted my problem with anger. I even told my congregation about my prayer "hit list" I use to pray for my enemies. My goal is to get people off of my hit list and onto my regular prayer list. One Wednesday night, I announced I had gotten everybody off my hit list, and the congregation broke into applause.

If the sermon is about a sin that is not a particular problem for me, I'll laugh and say, "I can preach a humdinger of a sermon on this, because this isn't my sin!" I create a non-judgmental mood, poking fun at my temptation to self-righteousness.

• *Identify recriminating guilt.* One temptation, as I've noted, is to motivate with guilt. In fact, people are so used to being motivated in this way, they can't imagine it any other way. They've gotten used to the oppressive sense of guilt, and they are happily surprised when the preacher suddenly turns the tables.

In seminars I teach around the country, I do one activity to help people see what kind of "prisons" they may be in: the prison of responsibility or of the past or of guilt. We look at twelve prisons in all. When I come to the section on guilt, I say, "None of you has shared your faith with a single person this week, and people are going to hell.

"Your devotional time is awful. Some of you aren't spending five minutes a day with the One who loves you and died on the cross for you.

"And how often do you really extend yourselves for neighbors, let alone your family?"

I go on and on until I see people squirm. Some look ill as I pound on them for what they know is all too true. But then I deliver the punch line: "What you're feeling right now is guilt pure and simple. It's how we are so often motivated. We beat ourselves until we feel utterly lousy. But friends, let us remember, we live in Christ. We don't have to live in the prison of self-recrimination anymore."

That's when people sit up, and I can nearly hear them say, "Oh yes, I understand!" And for the first time, many of them recognize how much they've been motivated by guilt. Once that motivation has been unmasked, people are in a much better position to respond appropriately — not merely out of guilt.

I will also make sure people know how the hard sermon is framed. If I have to spend most of my time talking about some sin, I will at some point in the sermon say, "Now, remember in everything I say, Christ died for you. I can only speak this word because we've already been accepted by him."

● *Speak a gracious repentance.* We have to be careful how we call others to repentance. I used to say, "Confession is saying, 'I'm sorry I spilled the milk,' and repentance is cleaning up the milk." I've realized two things, however.

First, people can't always clean up the milk. Some have made messes they can't wipe up as if nothing happened. Women have had abortions that can never be taken back. Men have committed adultery that can't be undone. People have divorced and remarried, then divorced and remarried again, leaving children with wounds that will never fully heal. Christians have spoken words that have ruined reputations and divided churches. Although apologies are in order, often people have to live with spiritual scars.

Second, such a view of preaching easily turns repentance into another work. When that happens, people will be driven to despair. They seek with all their might to do the right thing they promised in an act of contrition, but they will inevitably fail in some way. Then they will wallow in guilt rather than go to God, because they are ashamed of facing the one to whom they made such glowing promises.

Michael Quoist, author of *Prayers* (Sheed & Ward, 1985), described his own experience of this dynamic. Once when he felt in despair about his own Christian walk, he prayed to God something like, "I've sinned, Lord. I've played with it. I've fondled it. It's chased me like a dog. I can't go on."

Then God, he writes, spoke to him, in words to this effect: "Look up, child. Did you think I stopped loving you? The trouble is you trusted in yourself instead of me. It's not falling in the mud that's the worst; it's the staying there."

Calling to repentance doesn't mean calling people to straighten out every wrong they've committed. Repentance means agreeing with God about who he is, who you are, what you've done, and what needs to be changed. No more, no less. The paradox of grace is that we are closer to holiness if we trust God's mercy than if we try to be perfectly holy.

• *Start with milk.* If people are miserable sinners, then we've got to accept them where they are. This is an old principle: we can't give them meat until they've learned to drink milk.

For instance, when I challenge people to establish a devotional life, I give them a moderate goal to begin with: two or three minutes in the morning. And then I'll say, "Don't you dare increase that! Pray the Lord's Prayer, read a few verses of Scripture, and stop. If you want to do more, come and talk to me."

That way I take the pressure off. Instead of challenging them to an hour a day, a challenge that will leave the majority feeling defeated and unworthy, I start slow and build on their feelings of accomplishment.

As I often say, when a dog plays checkers, you don't criticize his game. You're just glad he's playing.

• *Let some people off the hook.* Sometimes you have to make it clear that you are not, in fact, singling someone out.

One man in the congregation was an activist for family issues. He had paid a big price for that, giving up time and money and peace of mind as he battled secular authorities about the integrity of the family. In one sermon, I was making a point about how we needed to love each other, that we shouldn't be adversarial when we deal with non-Christians. I realized that maybe he was thinking I was talking about him.

So I stopped in the sermon, turned to him, and said, "Jack, I'm not talking about you. What you're doing has cost you a lot, and I'm proud of you."

Sometimes you have to give people permission to heal first before they start marching in the Lord's army. The church I pastored in Key Biscayne was a healing church. People came to us who had been beaten up by sin and by religious institutions, and they needed a safe place. Many weren't ready to hear the hard side of the gospel. They needed comfort, love, and encouragement.

Periodically during sermons, I would single such people out: "If you've recently met Christ, if your life is still in complete shambles, don't worry about what I'm about to say. Your job for the time being is to get to know your loving Savior. There will be time enough for you to do something for him. As for those who've known Christ for some time . . ."

One man who eventually became a church leader told me, "Thank you for just letting me sit when I came here. For five years that was all I could do."

From Judgment to Love

A fellow preacher told this story: During his military campaigns, Alexander the Great held judgment day once a week. Those accused of cowardice were brought before him, and if found guilty, they were executed on the spot.

One day the guards brought before Alexander a young man who reportedly fled the battle and hid behind a rock. For some reason, observers said, as he heard the accusations against the young man, Alexander's face softened. Perhaps he was thinking about the soldier's girlfriend back home, about the children he would one day have.

"Son, what is your name?" the great commander asked.

"Alexander, sir," the young man replied.

The general's demeanor changed, his eyes flashed with anger. Stepping down from the judgment seat, he picked up the cowardly soldier and threw him to the ground. "Young man, either change your name or change your ways."

Unfortunately, that type of harsh attitude is what characterizes much of prophetic preaching today: "Christian: change your name or change your ways!" That will only produce more guilt and ineffectual Christian lives.

Instead, I want to foster an attitude of love, a love that wants to see people be their best and a love that cares for them where they are.

I learned something about this from John Stanton. Every Saturday when he pastored Westmont Presbyterian Church in Johnstown, Pennsylvania, he would go to the empty sanctuary and pray. One by one he would stand behind the pews, lay his hand on them, and pray for the person who would sit there the next day.

I did that for a number of years myself. And I found that as much as anything else, it developed in me a love for my people. Then preaching the hard side wasn't so harsh. No, it's never been a piece of cake. But neither has it turned into a sour apple.

To put it simply, by God's power, hard preaching on hard themes has been a means of grace for this pastor and his people.

*When we go through extended pain, we will often have to
preach about things we don't resonate with at the time.*
— *Haddon Robinson*

CHAPTER EIGHT

When You're
in Pain

Denver Seminary was hit with three lawsuits in the late 1980s. In
one case, a former student had sexually molested a boy, and the
family sued the seminary. Two others involved a former professor
who had gotten inappropriately involved with a counselee.

For one of the cases, I had to give a deposition. I had no idea
what to expect, but I wasn't worried because neither I nor the
seminary had done anything improper. With our lawyer at my side,
I walked into the room where the deposition would take place,
where we met four lawyers from the prosecution.

The questioning began, and I quickly came to a frightening realization. The four lawyers across the table were ruthless, and my lawyer was out of his depth. They were wolves, and he was a lamb. This was the first time he had handled such a case, and he had not prepared me for what happens at a deposition.

Only later did I learn the legal strategy behind such depositions. The prosecution knows that even if you are innocent, law suits can bring financial ruin. Insurance companies are wary of juries, and they stand to pay out $100,000 even if you win your case. So they're often willing to settle out of court even if you're innocent.

All the action, then, takes place in the depositions. That's where the prosecution tries to strike you with fear and make you settle out of court.

In my case, they did a good job of it. My deposition lasted two days. The first day prosecution lawyers grilled me for nine hours with question after question, doing everything they could to cast my answers into a negative light, twisting my motives, questioning my integrity.

Since then I have talked to others who have endured a deposition, and they have said it was the worst experience of their lives. It certainly was for me.

But that was only the beginning. The seminary's insurance company at one point said I personally wasn't covered by the school's policy. (I was also named in the suit). At one point, my lawyer (my new lawyer!) said, "They don't have a good case against us." But he knew that in this day anything can happen in court, so ten minutes later he advised, "You ought to take all your assets and put them in your wife's name. They can still get them, but it makes it harder." So our retirement savings all went in Bonnie's name.

Meanwhile, a former employee of Denver Seminary began to spread untruths about me throughout the community, which damaged my reputation. I had no effective way to respond.

The pain Bonnie and I suffered during those months was devastating. Frankly, I didn't respond well. Like the apostle Paul, I struggled with "conflicts on the outside, fears within." And yet I had to keep preaching, at chapel, in conventions and churches where I had been scheduled for months and years in advance, and later as interim pastor at Grace Chapel in Massachusetts.

All pastors go through times when they must preach through pain. How do you preach when you don't feel like it — when you're distracted, unable to focus, when your family is in turmoil or your health is failing or detractors in the church are launching artillery rounds in your direction, when you're going through loneliness or feelings of failure?

Dangers in the Tunnel

Going through extended times of pain feels like walking a dark, cold, damp tunnel. The tunnel of a preacher's pain has some unique dangers.

First, we can end up using the pulpit for self-therapy. One's style of preaching can change during a crisis. Often, along the way, a suffering pastor preaches a sermon that is nine-tenths his painful story and one-tenth Bible. Listeners identify with the sermon and are moved.

The pastor hears a favorable response to the message, and the next week, because it's difficult to study at such a time, he decides once again to share from his heart. The message is based primarily on his experience, with a sprinkling of Scripture thrown in. Again listeners respond warmly.

Soon he sets a pattern. He is now in danger of preaching weekly from his experience rather than from the Bible. Instead of experiencing what he preaches, he is preaching what he experiences. Preaching becomes a catharsis for his pain.

You cannot make the pulpit a place for self-therapy very often without paying a penalty. Parishioners don't come to church every Sunday to hear the wrestlings of the pastor's soul. They're not unsympathetic, but after a while the weekly service becomes an emotional downer. People don't follow for long leaders who can't handle their emotions.

Another danger is using the pulpit as a sniper's perch. If our pain comes from a church conflict, the temptation is strong to use the pulpit to take a bead on opponents.

Let's say Deacon Bill Jones is out to get the pastor. In the sermon the pastor quotes the verse "Alexander the metalworker did me a great deal of harm."

"We all know what this is like," the pastor says. "There will be times when we want to go forward for God, and others will stand up in a business meeting and call the congregation back to the past. We need to follow God as did the apostle Paul, even when others try to block our way."

The pastor never mentions Bill Jones, but anyone in the know sees right through the comments. They'll be upset that the pastor used the pulpit as a weapon, especially if they feel Deacon Jones's opposition has merit.

If our church is in conflict, we have to take care that people can't read into our comments an attack we never intended.

Furthermore, we can fail to preach the full counsel of God. When we're in pain, we tend to think everyone is in pain. Even if we never mention our personal troubles, our preaching can become strictly an ambulance service focused on crises. Those who are healthy, moving up in their businesses, and feeling strong in the Lord, won't get much out of our preaching.

I went with my daughter to the movie *Wall Street* several years ago. Gordon Gecko, one of the key characters in the film, was a successful, even ruthless, player of the stock market.

After the movie, my daughter said, "Daddy, what if Gecko said to you, 'You're a Christian. What can you say to somebody like me? You have one hour to give me your best shot.' What would you say to him?"

She gave me pause. Sometimes the church doesn't know what to say to the Gordon Geckos of the world. We can only speak to them, it seems, after they have fallen. Yet, the Scriptures speak both to the weak and the strong. I don't intentionally ignore successful people in sermons, but that's easy to do when I'm in pain.

When we're suffering, we need others to remind us there are more preaching themes than depravity, grace, faith, and prayer. We need to preach also about righteousness, God's sovereignty, justice, outreach, and other fundamental doctrines. Just because some themes aren't feeding me at the moment doesn't mean they no longer are good food for others.

Preaching in the Dark

Some painful situations are naturally shared with the congregation: the death of a loved one, serious illness.

Other situations require discretion: financial problems, marriage stress, conflict on the board, a moral lapse. Even if we never mention such problems, our preaching changes as we walk the tunnel of pain.

As I was living through this intense period of pain at Denver Seminary, several people said they sensed more tenderness and sympathy in my preaching. That is certainly what I felt. If anything good for me came out of this painful time, it was the overwhelming sense of my need of God. I felt completely vulnerable. Although I was not guilty of any legal negligence or failure, I felt more in need of grace than ever.

When prosecutors hammered away at my motives and conduct, when others spread slander and rumors, it forced me to examine my life. I looked into my heart and saw that in spite of my legal innocence, I was like every other person, a sinful human being with impure motives much of the time, in need of God's grace all the time.

One sermon I preached while "in the tunnel" was the parable of the Prodigal Son. I talked about the Father: not worrying about his dignity, his heart filled with grace and acceptance, he ran to meet his son, the prodigal. "I just want you to know the Father is running to meet you," I told the congregation. "His arms are open wide, and he's not angry with you. More than anything else, he just wants you to come home. He says, 'I don't care if you're covered with mud and manure. I don't care how you smell. Welcome home! Welcome home!'

"If that's where you are this morning, I want to welcome you home. Come up here, and let me welcome you home."

One woman answering that appeal told me, "I've been in

church and heard invitations all my life. There is no way in the world I would go forward in a church. But I wanted to come. I wanted to be welcomed home."

During a conversation with a work associate, I shared the ideas from that sermon, and she began to weep. She is a fairly controlled person. "Never in my life," she said, "have I felt the full meaning of that parable."

Such reactions weren't due to any new preaching technique or profound insight on my part. I had experienced God's grace anew, and the power of that grace simply came through, without my consciously striving for it to happen.

Pain and the Pastor's Family

Our families share the darkness when we walk through pain. They see us at our best and worst. And then they see us stand before a congregation and preach the will of God. Our families won't question our sincerity if we avoid two mistakes.

First, don't imply that what ought to be actually is in your life. A preacher's responsibility is to declare what Christians ought to do. We teach others to read their Bibles and pray daily, have family devotions regularly, share their faith at every opportunity, pray for our nation's leaders, give as much as possible to missions, sacrifice for others, live unselfishly. At the same time, few if any pastors do *all* that Christians ought to do.

That's no surprise and no problem, if we're honest. It's only a problem if we imply otherwise. And it becomes a major problem if we have pain in the family.

If we suggest in our preaching that we have all the answers, that our faith is unshakable, that "all you need is Jesus," that we have it all together, and meanwhile our family sees us in doubt, anger, and confusion at home, they'll conclude we are hypocrites and doubt the reality of what we preach.

When I went through my experience at Denver, I was not a model of unwavering, unquestioning faith. I went through times of deep discouragement. My family saw me go through those times. If I had stood up Sunday after Sunday and said, "When you go through a trial, put your faith in God. Don't waver. Don't doubt," I would have lost a lot of credibility with them.

Better to say something like, "When we go through trials, we need to put our faith in God. At times we may waver. At times we may doubt. But we need to pursue faith. Only by faith in the Lord Jesus Christ can we keep our footing when we feel we're slipping."

Second, don't illustrate with your best moments and imply that's the norm. For several months, a pastor suffers unrelenting attacks from his elder board. It gets the best of him. Embittered, he comes home each night and at dinner complains to his family about the latest criticism and speaks disparagingly about various board members.

One night in the middle of the conflict, by contrast, he says to the family, "We need to pray for the board members and their families. No doubt they have pain in their lives that is causing them to be negative toward me."

The next day and for weeks to come, however, the pastor falls back into bitter comments when with the family.

Later the pastor preaches on praying for enemies and illustrates by saying, "As you may know, we went through some disagreements here at the church several months ago. During that time God helped my family to sit together at the dinner table and pray for those who had personally attacked us."

He's telling the truth, but he's implying that the ideal was the norm. He probably isn't intentionally trying to mislead the congregation; he's trying to inspire them with an example of doing what is right. But he is in danger of embittering his family, who have seen his ambivalent behavior.

Preaching When You Don't Feel Like It

Pain makes it hard to concentrate on anything but our problems. It distracts us, confuses us, and saps our energies, leaving us feeling like we don't want to prepare sermons or get "up" for preaching. Preaching through pain requires that we do two things: compartmentalize and filter.

When we go through extended pain, we will often have to

preach about things we don't resonate with at the time. We will talk about the sovereignty of God when we feel everything is out of control, or about confidence in God when we ourselves are struggling with unanswered prayer.

At those times, we need to fulfill the calling to preach the Bible. We preach what the Bible says, not what we feel. We, on our own authority, based on our own experiences, may not be able to say, "All things work together for good," but we can say, "God's Word says that all things work together for good."

In a sense, sometimes we have to compartmentalize our experience and feelings. At those times, we may not interact personally with the text or illustrate from our own lives. That's reality.

At such times, it's appropriate to recognize publicly the ambivalence between the text's great promise and the human condition. If you're preaching through the Psalms and come to a place where the psalmist says, "The Lord has rewarded me for my integrity, for the cleanness of my hands in his sight," but you feel the weight of your sin, you can say: "Perhaps you feel like the psalmist today. You're not perfect, but you're forgiven, and you're trying by his grace to walk with God. You feel like praising God that he is a God of justice who rewards the righteous and repays the wicked. You can do that. Others of you will feel a great sense of failure—I know I often do. You can't say with integrity, 'I've served you with my whole heart.' You're feeling instead like the 'chief of sinners.' So this psalm doesn't express how you're feeling today. Still, the psalmist is at a place all of us want to be at times. So let's all listen in, and see what we can learn."

We also need to filter. If we always keep a sermon "out there," we eventually lose our sense of authenticity. If we just keep hammering together what I call "dog house" sermons — *let's see, I need three points that begin with the letter* T — without living in those sermons, we get hollow. On occasion we need to filter our preaching through our experiences, choosing sermon texts that resonate with what we feel, sharing some of the tough lessons we are learning even if we never tell the story behind them.

In years past, when I would read the parable of the sheep and the goats at the judgment, I felt like a sheep. I had faith in Christ; I visited friends in the hospital; I gave to World Vision.

When I went through the tunnel, I felt totally unworthy of salvation. For the first time, I read that parable and noticed that after Christ commended the sheep, they responded, "Who, me?" They didn't know they were sheep. They didn't feel like sheep.

I came to the conclusion that if I get into heaven, it's because God says I'm a sheep, not because I feel like I'm doing what sheep do. It's all grace.

I began preaching that passage. I felt I had to preach it because it reflected my heart; it made some sense of what I was going through.

After the three lawsuits against Denver Seminary were settled, my lawyer met with the faculty to explain all he could not explain during the trials. He told the faculty, for example, that the president of another seminary had gone over all the testimony and seminary records. He testified that he would have handled the situations just as I had. After all the facts came out, some of the faculty contacted me to say that meeting had vindicated me.

The whole thing is behind me now, though my life will never be the same. And neither will my preaching.

PART THREE

External Pressures

We've got to become pastors if we want our people to become congregations.

— *William Willimon*

How an Audience Becomes a Congregation

The first Christmas I was at Duke, during the time I was not preaching regularly, my wife and I attended a local church. That year Christmas fell on a Sunday. Our son was 2 years old, so we dressed him up in his spanking new Christmas clothes and headed jubilantly off to church. We looked forward to the service with anticipation.

But when the pastor stood up to welcome the congregation, he said, "Today is the first time in a while that Christmas has fallen on Sunday. It would have been unfair to ask the choir to sing this morning, this being a big family day and all, so they won't be singing.

"I'm not really going to preach this morning either. Instead, I've got a little story to share with you. You know, I'm amazed you're here this morning. Most of you have guests from out of town. Coming today was such an inconvenience."

"I'm leaving," my wife whispered to me. "You stay with the baby, if you want." She was annoyed the pastor hadn't dignified his congregation with preparation, and she stomped out.

I couldn't be too critical of this minister, however. I remembered many Christmas Eve services when I had scrambled to put together a service only to find no one showed up. Still, he had taken for granted that his people would be uncommitted, that they would be as fickle as a Hollywood audience.

Certainly, the dynamics of the modern congregation are discouraging. Sunday has become just another day to consume. Those who do attend worship nearly demand to be entertained.

But they are still a Christian congregation, and we do well to treat them as such, though how we do that is often hard to discern. How do we preach to such a crowd week after week? How can we move them from being individualistic consumers to a community of saints responding to God's Word?

Frustrations

A number of factors inhibit our Sunday morning crowds from being a congregation, and the first is that our people have adopted many of the values of our consumer and leisure society.

We see this in people's lifestyles. One pastor in Colorado recently complained because of his congregation's weekend trips. His church is located in a suburb of Denver, and many in his congregation own condos in Breckenridge or Vail. Certain periods of the year — ski season, for example, which can run from early November to the middle of April — many otherwise steadfast members attend irregularly. Trying to sustain a sense of community is futile.

We also see consumerism in people's expectations. Not long

ago I attended a conference of lay people from a major denomination. When asked, "What do you want out of a sermon?" one of the conference participants said, "We want sermons that start us thinking about something in a new way."

In the name of intellectual stimulation, these people wanted to consume fresh ideas rather than being confronted with the old truths of Scripture. Their attitude reflects that of an audience, a consumerist mindset bent on being served.

Second, those attending have fewer strong ties to others in the church. In my last church, for those nearing retirement, the church was their social center. The crowd at a covered-dish social at church would also be the same at a downtown dinner party. If I would have asked them, "Who are your five best friends?" most would have named at least three from the church.

Even a generation ago, the majority attending our churches lived in the same town and got their mail from the same post office and shopped at the same general store. So much of their lives was shared together before they even arrived on Sunday morning.

To most of the younger crowd in my last congregation, however, church was only one of many stops along a busy highway. Many commuted twenty to thirty minutes, and they could not name even one close church friend.

Third, today's average churchgoer is largely unfamiliar with Christian speech. People arrive on Sunday morning without a working knowledge of Christianity. They hear our words without some fundamental assumptions of Scripture.

A woman recently complained to me about the youth group her 17-year-old daughter attends. Her daughter had said something like, "The Trinity is an outmoded concept. We don't need to think of God in such a complicated way anymore."

The youth leader had replied, "Well, that's wrong. That's not the way Christians look at it."

The girl's mother was deeply offended: how presumptuous of this youth pastor to tell her daughter she was wrong!

"Your daughter is extremely bright," I said after listening to this mother. "She's gotten a huge scholarship to the college of her choice. But she's ignorant and uninformed when it comes to basic Christian doctrine. As Christians, we're not here to say, 'I agree or disagree with that.' We're here to be instructed, to be inculturated into a very different way of looking at things."

Fourth, many people approach the sermon as consumers looking for good service. A few weeks prior to my first baccalaureate sermon at Duke, I pulled aside a few seniors I knew well and asked for their suggestions.

"Please talk about God," they said. "We're going to be told in the graduation speeches we're 'the hope of tomorrow.' But in the baccalaureate message, don't pull any punches."

Last year in doing so, however, I offended a graduate's father. I was talking about the uncertainty of young adults as they face the future. And then I said something like, "You should be uncertain, with the huge deficits we have run up, which you are going to have to pay for. You may have been raised by the most selfish generation ever to rule America. No wonder you're scared."

Afterwards, an angry father said to me, "I didn't pay $100,000 in tuition to hear someone tell me how bad I am."

Apparently he thought he didn't get his money's worth.

Attitude Check

Our fickle congregations can tempt us in two directions. On the one hand, we may pander to their consumerist mindset. We avoid the controversial, even if it's biblical, and we strive to make people feel good, designing the service so they're pumped up by the end.

On the other hand, cynicism can set in: "My people don't care about the gospel. They just want to be entertained, to feel good about their miserable little lives." So we preach without expecting any significant change.

A better response requires a fundamental shift in attitude. I've seen over the years that a congregation's behavior is sometimes deceptive. Though they have a long way to go, there are definite signs they yearn to become a congregation. Here are three attitudes I've developed to remind me of that.

First, I've developed an amazement when people do show up. There are a lot of other things people could be doing on Sunday morning. Many make sacrifices to get to church.

Last winter I was given an assignment by Duke's president to spend more time with students, so early on Sunday morning (2:30 A.M.) after a basketball game with Michigan, I hung out at a bonfire with several of them. I walked up to one student I knew, who was surprised to see me, and I said jokingly, "Good morning, David. I bet you won't be at chapel later this morning."

"It will be easier for me than it will be for you," he kidded me. "I'm used to this, and you aren't!"

"Oh, David," I retorted. "You're so young and arrogant!" We then spent a half-hour talking about his life. *I can't believe I'm here,* I thought. *In just a few hours, I'm supposed to preach.*

Later that morning, at five minutes to eleven, I was standing with the choir in the back of the sanctuary when in walked David.

"You're up!" I said in surprise.

"Yeah," he said, "and I look better than you do. And you probably got more sleep than I did."

Yeah, I thought. *And I didn't drink what you drank either.*

As he headed for the sanctuary, he said, "You better be good today."

When I think of the five-hundred reasons not to go to church, when I reflect upon how archaic preaching must seem to people — and how lousy I preach some days — I'm utterly amazed at the people who do show up consistently.

Second, I've learned to relish the serendipities of ministry. When something remarkable happens as a result of preaching, for instance, we're tempted to think, *Well, it's about time.* Instead, I want to be thankful, for God's Spirit has been at work creating faith and Christian community.

I once preached a sermon on sex, and the next week I received a call from a father.

"I don't know what kind of reaction you got from last Sunday's sermon," he said. "But I just want to tell you my 17-year-old son was there." I braced myself for shock and anger.

"Getting my son to church last week was such a hassle," he continued. "I physically forced him to come. When he arrived, he was angry and sat with his arms folded.

"I didn't hear much of your sermon because I was so busy watching my son. But when you started in on sex, his mouth dropped open. He was stunned that you would preach on such a topic. I was so proud that we were there. I was proud of you.

"When you finished, I didn't say a word. But on the way home, my son said, 'Gosh, was this sermon typical of him?' 'Yeah,' I replied. 'That's a typical Willimon sermon.' I lied — all your sermons are not that interesting — but I just want to thank you for what you said on Sunday."

That's the type of incident I want to be thankful for — sort of.

Finally, I treat those who have shown up for worship with pastoral respect. Many people are coming with burdens for which they are seeking God's help.

My first four years at Duke, I taught solely in the divinity school. It was the first time since graduate school I wasn't preaching, so I attended a local church. One Sunday I walked into the church sanctuary and sat beside a middle-aged woman. The organ was still playing the prelude, so I turned to her and asked how she was doing.

"Not so well," she replied. "My husband was killed last week."

"What?"

"A drunk driver killed him," she continued. "What makes his death so hard is that we were separated at the time."

"I'm so sorry." Taken back, I turned to greet an older man who had just sat down on the other side of me.

"George, how have you been?" I asked.

"I haven't been here in a month," he replied.

"Anything wrong?"

"Well, my mother died," he said. "It's just the worst thing that has ever happened to me. I miss her so much."

"I'm so sorry to hear that," I said.

Just then the service began, for which I was extremely grateful. I've never since presumed my listeners don't need and want the community created by the gospel.

Corporate Training

I'm constantly intrigued with Duke's basketball fans. As if on a timer, all the students in the gymnasium, when the opposing coach steps out of the locker room wearing a plaid sportscoat, begin shouting in unison, "Your coat sucks! Your coat sucks!"

How do 2,000 students know when to begin and what to shout? They're astute observers of the game; they've been trained.

To get our people to become a congregation will also require training. The centrifugal forces of our culture pulling our people apart are strong. We simply can't expect them to arrive on Sunday knowing what they're supposed to do.

I've learned that training them might be easier than we think. In one of the congregations I pastored, I was warned about a member who was considered a "hot head." A couple of months after I arrived, this man approached me after a service. "I just don't see it the way you told it this morning, Pastor," he said. "Maybe I missed something, but I don't think you're right."

I immediately got defensive. "Wally," I said, "I don't know exactly what you heard — "

"Wait a minute," he cut in. "I didn't ask you to take it back. I'm only saying I didn't understand and so I disagree. What kind of preacher are you, anyway? Someone who stands up and says something and then takes it back when someone disagrees?"

Later this man said, "You know, you get to read books all the time. You get to think about all these great things. I run a hardware store, and you can learn to run a hardware store in a year — I've being doing it for nineteen years.

"Sunday is the only time I can feel like a thinking person. A retired man who works with me and I sit down after we open the store on Monday and have a cup of coffee and talk about your sermon."

Wally, it turned out, wasn't a hot head, just a man who was impatient with preachers who didn't take their jobs seriously. I've never forgotten his comments. He gave me authorization to conduct business on Sunday morning. If a hardware store owner was interested in interacting with Sunday's sermon, I knew I could train others to do the same.

My first priority, then, is to preach a sermon that speaks about the gospel, not a speech that explores people's experiences. In the admirable attempt to be relevant, too many sermons I hear whitewash therapeutic solutions with biblical "principles," where the Bible ends up sounding like the latest rage of popular psychology.

Furthermore, my sermon will not be a lecture or a political speech. When we give such sermons, we merely reinforce people's habits of mind. They come to expect that a sermon is, first and foremost, about what goes on in their worlds.

Instead, a sermon is, first and foremost, about Jesus Christ and what he has done for us and what he calls us to do for him and one another. I want to preach so that people come expecting to hear a word about that. In short, I want to train them to ask not "Was this relevant to the latest things going in my world?" but "Was this sermon faithful to the revealed text of Scripture?"

In a recent sermon on a passage in Ephesians, which was about not letting filthy talk come out of our mouths, I said, "You know me. I like to preach on the big stuff — sex, war, racism — the large sins. What Ephesians is saying this morning, however, seems so petty. One reason I like to go for the big sins is because it's easier to talk about South Africa's racial problems than what happened at the last board meeting."

I contrasted what I wanted to preach on with the text's clearly stated aims. Then I proceeded to preach the passage I had been given. I sent a clear message that what I preach isn't necessarily my idea; I am bound by Scripture, and this is what people are getting.

If my first task is to get people to hear the Word (versus human words), my second task is to get people to react to the Word, to get them talking about that Word. I recently preached a sermon on Romans 1. The apostle Paul introduces Romans with a laundry list of sins: envy, malice, murder, and the like. After referring to the passage, I gave some statistics on the number of violent crimes in North Carolina.

Then I said, "Paul gives us his list of devastating statistics. But then, after setting up this dismal picture of 'God left us,' he moves to 'God came to us.' "

I illustrated with a story from the *Durham Morning Herald* about a black woman whose brother was shot and killed as he was going to cook a turkey for some poor people before Christmas. Along with the article was a heart-wrenching picture of this woman lying prostrate on the sidewalk, screaming with grief.

The article reported her words: "It ain't supposed to be this way." The mother of this man and woman was also there, holding a Bible. Some friends were there as well, and they were quoted as saying, "We're going to find out who did this. We're going to kill him!"

But pointing to the Bible, the mother said, "No, this is my weapon."

I closed the sermon by saying, "I want you to listen to these two women and remember two things: first, it ain't supposed to be like this; we created this mess, and we can change it through Jesus. Second, the Bible is our weapon, not rockets or guns."

I wanted my listeners to walk out of the service saying, "I found that terribly depressing," or "That seemed sort of simplistic. Does Willimon really believe the answer to the crime rate in Durham is Jesus — just accept Jesus and everything will be okay?" So I preached to get a reaction, to get people thinking and talking.

After an exceptional movie or concert, people walk out and find themselves talking to complete strangers because both experienced something so powerful. I want that same thing to happen as a result of my preaching, even if my hyperboles are sometimes misunderstood.

I may want to assault people's experiences with the outrageous truths of the gospel. As Martin Luther said, "The sermon is the thunderbolt hurled from heaven to blast unrepentant sinners but more so righteous saints."

Pastoral Training

Training our listeners to expect something more out of Sunday morning than consumption, however, assumes we understand the world in which they live. This requires our own training. To put it another way, we've got to become pastors if we want our people to become congregations.

I once visited a frail woman from my congregation at her place of employment. The two men she worked for were brothers, both loud and obnoxious. The office air was clouded with cigar smoke. I gasped for air as I walked into the office.

As I was talking to this woman at her desk, one of the brothers shouted from his office, "Where the hell is that report?"

"I don't know where that G-- d--- report is," shouted the other brother, sitting in his office across the hall. "You get the report."

"Peggy," one of them yelled, "find that damn report."

"I'm talking with my minister," she answered. "I'll get it for you in a couple of minutes."

"I don't care who you're talking to," one of them said. "Just get us the G-- d--- report!"

She turned to me and said, "This is what I live with eight hours a day, five days a week. I can already hear them yelling all the way down the hall as I arrive each morning."

Several months after my visit, I still couldn't shake the memory of her working environment.

Pastoral visitation is great training for the preacher; it's sermon preparation. Many times, when I've struggled with a passage during the week, I've suddenly gotten an "Ah ha!" connection while listening to someone in his living room. It chastens my language and provides me a window into people's souls.

Our pastoral care will affect how we preach. After I was at Duke for a couple of years, my wife told me she thought my sermons seemed less intellectual. *What?* I thought. *How could that be true? I'm preaching in an academic setting.*

But she was right. When I was pastor of North Side Methodist Church, a blue-collar congregation, I would say, "Today I'm going to tell you about the significance of Christian baptism. First, . . ." There, I explained more, attempting overtly to educate them as I preached.

At Duke, however, my impression is that my listeners do not come to Duke Chapel to hear another lecture. The mistake most guest preachers make here is to think, *Oooh, I'm at a university. I've got to appeal to their minds.* The Duke crowd reacts negatively, though, when a preacher tries to compete with them intellectually. I've overheard faculty say, "Who does he think he is? I didn't come to hear a third-rate academic."

So when I preach at Duke, I intentionally go for the gut; I want my listeners to feel truth. That's what they want, as well. Last Sunday a black soloist sang, "His Eye Is on the Sparrow," and I looked down from my vantage point and saw a well-credentialed Duke history professor fumbling for his handkerchief.

More than a Rotary Club

What I'm saying here briefly I explore more thoroughly in my book, *Peculiar Speech: Preaching to the Baptized* (Eerdmans, 1992). Yet a lot of what I'm driving at can be summarized in a story.

A former student of mine was pastoring a small congregation, and one Sunday, just before the pastoral prayer, he asked the congregation for prayer requests.

A woman named Mary stood up: "Joe left us this week, and he's gone for good. I don't know how the girls and I are going to survive. Please pray for us."

The pastor was stunned. How could anybody be so tacky as to lay such a request on people during worship? *She's breaking the rules,* he thought. *We only pray publicly for gall bladder operations or hospital-ized mother-in-laws. This is too messy.*

"Well, honey," an older woman piped up, interrupting his thoughts, "I don't know that we have to pray for that. When my husband left me, the way I survived was through some of the people right here in this church. We can help you."

Flabbergasted, the minister listened in silence.

"But what am I going to do?" said Mary. "I've only got a high school diploma. I've never worked in my life."

"This is weird that this should happen now," said a man seated further back. "I'm looking for a new employee. I can't pay a lot for this position, but it would be enough to keep going. No experience is really necessary, and we would train you for the job. Why don't you talk to me afterwards."

The pastor recovered enough to pray and then finished out the morning service.

The next Sunday, however, when the pastor stood up in the pulpit, he said, "Last Sunday, when Mary requested prayer, was a holy moment for us. Mary made us a church. I'm not sure we were a church before she laid that on us.

"I've often wondered if going to seminary and becoming a minister was worth it. I've questioned whether church was no more than a glorified Rotary Club or Women's Garden Club. I want to speak for all of us and say, 'Thank you, Mary,' and 'Thank you, God,' for making us a church."

My student friend was a touch too humble, because it was his preaching and pastoring — the age-old tasks of the minister —that nurtured virtues that sprang forth in that service. It's just one small example of what can happen in church: it really can become a congregation.

Sermon ideas ignite when the flint of people's problems strikes the steel of God's Word.

— *Haddon Robinson*

CHAPTER TEN

Having Something to Say

Preaching well is hard work. We're expected to be witty, warm, and wise. And then next week, we have to do it again.

The great science fiction writer H. G. Wells reportedly said most people think only once or twice in a lifetime, whereas he had made an international reputation by thinking once or twice a year.

Lots of pastors have to think once (or more) a week! More often than we would like to admit, we begin preparing a sermon with the feeling not that we have something to say but that we have to say something. Only one time in twenty do I start a sermon with the feeling that this sermon is going well. The creative process is accompanied with a feeling of ambiguity, uncertainty, of trying to make the unknown known.

Like the homemaker whose goal of three nutritious meals a day is complicated by toddlers making messes, demands of a part-time job, overflowing baskets of laundry, and a phone that won't stop ringing, the multiple demands of pastoral life make fresh thinking and sermon writing even more difficult.

People never die at convenient times. The administrative load preoccupies pastors with scores of details that won't go away. Emotional weariness from dealing with people problems drains creative energies. And speaking several times weekly outstrips a person's capacity to assimilate truth fully into one's life.

Just as savvy homemakers find resourceful ways to feed their families — a deft combination of ten-minute recipes, healthy snacks, a microwave special, and a few full-course evening feasts — pastors, too, can find ways to keep tasty and balanced spiritual meals on the table.

Distinct Phases

When we feel we don't have anything to say in a sermon, it's usually because we've gotten ahead of ourselves. We're thinking about the sermon before we've understood the text. Instead, we need to divide our sermon preparation into two distinct phases.

1. What am I going to say? I start the process by focusing on content, not delivery. Approaching a text with the attitude *How am I going to get a sermon out of this?* pollutes the process. We can end up manipulating the text for the purposes of an outline instead of first trying to observe, interpret, and appreciate the text.

For one message based on the story of Christ calming the storm, I began my study assuming my sermon's main idea would be that we can count on Christ to calm the wind and waves in our lives. But as I studied the text, I realized I couldn't promise people they would never sink just because Christ was with them in the storms of life.

This passage has to be seen in its broader context. Jesus has called the disciples and told them about the nature of his kingdom: it will start small but spread wide. In that early stage, everything depended on the men in that boat — Jesus and the disciples. If they go under, the kingdom is gone. The point of the passage is that those who have committed everything to Christ's cause can know that the kingdom will ultimately triumph because of the power of the King. This is an eternal truth that shifts the emphasis from the personal storms in my life and whether I will sink to the eternal kingdom that will never fail.

If I promised that Christ would calm every storm, I would have twisted the text to say what I wanted. Instead I preached what the text taught me.

I have learned to let understanding the text dominate the sermon process early and later let sermonizing dominate. I have more material than I can preach when I first try to understand and interpret a text for its own sake. I ask, *What is the biblical writer doing?* Then I study the context for the flow of thought. (I usually get more preachable insights from context than from studying the grammar and word structure of the original language.)

By studying the context, I came up with a major lead for a sermon on 1 Peter 5. "To the elders among you," writes Peter, "I appeal as a fellow elder, a witness of Christ's sufferings and one who also will share in the glory to be revealed" (v. 1). In my study, I found the theme of suffering accompanied by glory runs throughout 1 Peter. Whether in marriage, government, family — or church — when we suffer for Christ, we experience the glory of Christ. My sermon therefore pointed to this theme as it applied to leaders in the church.

2. *How am I going to say it?* In this phase, I move to the communication question. How will I get the ideas I've uncovered in the passage across to people in a way that interests, informs, motivates, and changes them? Out of all that I could say about this passage, what will I choose to say?

This part of the process can also provide us with something significant to say. Early on I ask, *Which of the following tacks is the biblical writer taking here: Is he primarily (a) explaining, (b) proving, or (c) applying?*

If the passage majors in explanation, then my sermon will major in teaching. In the parable of the Pharisee and the tax collector (Luke 18:9–14), the primary purpose of this passage is to teach that the person who sees God as God and humbles himself before him is justified and exalted, and the person who exalts himself before God remains in his sins.

Accordingly, my sermon majors in explanation not exhortation. I dig beneath the assumptions we have about Pharisees and tax collectors, helping my listeners get into the minds of these two men. What did they think about themselves? What did others think about them? How would these roles look today? I talked about the nature of the sins of hypocrisy, self-righteousness, and disobedience.

One of the best ways to overcome "sermon block" is to think through *What's hard to believe about this passage?*

We can underrate the need to prove the truth of a text. Even if there isn't a skeptical bone in our body, we need to ask, *Will those who hear me believe this? Does this conform to my and their experience? If not, why not?*

Our experience doesn't govern the Bible, but we need to explain perceived discrepancies between what the Bible says and our reality. Suppose someone hears the passage, "If two of you on earth agree on anything, it will be done for you." She wonders, *What if I want a blue Cadillac? If I can get two of the elders to agree with me in prayer, is that a done deal?* Like most people, she questions, *Do I believe that?*

In my sermon, I try to be an advocate for that person. She won't raise her hand and interrupt me, but like most people in the pews today, she listens to sermons with a keen sense of skepticism. The preacher who ignores that is ignoring reality. C. S. Lewis has been popular in recent decades largely because he deals with the "Is this really true?" question. He assumed people needed to be convinced.

Good ideas for preaching also emerge as we apply the Bible's truths to people's lives. Sermon ideas ignite when the flint of people's problems strikes the steel of God's Word.

Sometimes we can't come up with much to say because our thinking is too steely; it's all God's Word, but we don't link it to specific situations in contemporary life. Other times we come up short because we're too flinty; we're people-oriented, but we lack the authoritative content that only Scripture can bring.

But we almost always spark a preaching flame if we strike those two elements together. So part of my preparation is to ask these application questions: What difference does this make? What are the implications for our lives in this text? If someone takes this truth seriously and tries to live it on Monday morning, how will he or she live differently?

Kitchen Helpers

Like labor-saving devices in the kitchen, there are ways to write a sermon that can relieve the pressure of finding something to say. Here are six "kitchen helpers."

1. Develop a preaching calendar. Many pastors set up a plan for what they will preach over the next quarter, half-year, or year. We can take a retreat for several days and ask ourselves what the needs of the congregation are, what subjects we sense God impressing on our hearts, what themes we have an avid interest in.

A preaching calendar doesn't have to confine us. If some brilliant stroke from God strikes us, we can always change our preaching plans. But if not, when we walk into the study, we have a sense of well-thought-through, well-prayed-through direction.

My calendars have been based primarily on expository series through complete books of the Bible (which provides more than enough grist for any mill).

Once a calendar is set, we can set up file folders for each series of sermons, which become repositories for the relevant material we come across in the weeks and months before the sermons are preached. When the time finally comes to begin preparing the sermon, we already have a file of illustrations, quotes, insights.

2. Work on sermons in ten-day cycles. The purpose of a longer cycle is to provide simmer time.

On the Thursday ten days prior to the Sunday I will preach, I do my exegetical study. I read the text and think about it till I hit a wall. Then I write down what is holding me up: What words don't

I understand? What issues can't I solve? What ideas don't make sense? If you can't state specifically where your problems are, you won't get answers.

Thus, ten days before I preach a sermon, I know what I need to be thinking about, which I do while driving the car, taking a shower, or lying awake at night. This also directs my reading. I know where the gaps in my understanding are, and I can more quickly find the answers. I can cull twenty commentaries in an hour if I know the key questions.

Often, when I sit down to resume study the following Tuesday, the issues in the passage are much clearer. I wonder, *What in the world was I so hung up about?*

When I preached a sermon on the seven churches of Revelation, I grew curious about the seven cities and how they affected the churches. I did some extra research that added significant insights. If I had been writing this sermon the day or two before preaching, I couldn't have done that.

My next study time in the cycle is five days later, on Tuesday, when I finish up my exegetical work and organize the sermon. By the end of Tuesday I want at least to have the sermon's homiletical skeleton and introduction completed. I may also have begun shaping the main movements.

My final writing installment takes place on Friday. I finish writing and actually have time to rearrange and polish.

3. Get double duty off study. Duane Litfin, president of Wheaton College, first introduced me to the idea of preparing two sermons from research on one preaching passage. When he was pastoring in Memphis, if his Sunday morning message primarily explained or proved the truth of a passage, on Sunday night he focused on application. Or, on Sunday night he developed a subtheme of a passage that couldn't be given justice in the Sunday morning message. In Philippians 2:1–11, for example, he might preach in the morning on Christlike humility and on Sunday night, the doctrine of Christ's humanity.

4. Think visually. Think of words on a spectrum, with abstract words and ideas at the top of the ladder and concrete ideas at the bottom. Scholars climb up the ladder of abstraction; communicators step down to get as close to specifics as possible.

When I have an idea without a specific picture in my mind, nothing interesting happens in me. But my mind starts to roll when I have an image.

When I study a text, I ask, *What image was in the biblical writer's mind as he wrote this?* If the subject is reconciliation, he didn't write about some abstract doctrine; he was thinking about enemies who made peace. As I study such a passage, I pose questions that keep me close to real life: *What's it like to have an enemy? Why is it so hard to make peace?* I'll think about countries in Europe, where people who have lived together for decades suddenly begin killing each other. What happens when neighbors turn into enemies?

I don't think about abstract ideas like "parenting." I think of bouncing a baby on my knee, of getting up in the middle of the night and staggering to a crib, to a child who won't stop crying, and of the feelings of love and anger that go along with all this.

5. *Work on a sermon out loud.* My family learned that if they walk by my office and hear me mumbling, I'm working on a sermon. I get in imaginary conversations with people I want the sermon to help:

"Robinson, you say God wants us to love our neighbors, but what do you do when you go to wash their feet and they kick you in the mouth? How many times do you get kicked before you say, 'Forget it'?"

"You have to get kicked three times," I'll continue out loud to myself, "and then you can break his toes. No, I wouldn't say that. What would I say?"

Working through a sermon aloud helps crystallize our thinking. It also gives us a feel for the flow of thought in the text.

6. *Borrow.* God doesn't give us any points for originality. He gives points for being faithful and clear. To have sitting on our shelves books from the great teachers of the world, people who have spent years of their lives studying a book like Romans, and not use them is to deny the many contributions of Christ's church. To think that in three hours of exegesis we're going to match the

insights of those who've spent years studying a book is a mistake.

But save commentaries for later in the process. If we go to the commentaries too quickly, they frame our thoughts. But once I have read through a passage and know where my difficulties lie, commentators become my teachers.

Tributaries for High-Water Preaching

I have developed habits that help me collect material for sermons on an ongoing basis (not just for the sermon I will be preaching this Sunday). They are tributaries for high-water preaching.

First, I observe and interpret daily life. Helmut Thielicke said, "The world is God's picture book." We can waste a lot of experiences. There are lessons in every day's events, in things as mundane as getting stuck in traffic or hearing a joke.

This is especially so when something happens that touches us emotionally, either positively or negatively. Even if I don't immediately grasp its significance, I write the anecdote down on a 3x5 card and reflect on it. It's a piece of life that someday will fit some insight, illustration, or sermon.

Reading books and magazines and watching movies and television — even commercials — is another way of observing life.

I watched a foreign film, *Jean de Florette*, which begins with a city dweller inheriting a farm, moving to the country, and trying to learn farming from books.

Wanting the farm for themselves, some unscrupulous neighbors block a spring that irrigates the farm. The new owner, unaware that he owns spring water, prays for rain. Storm clouds gather, but the rain falls on the other side of the mountain, never watering his land. Eventually the man dies, and the corrupt men buy his farm for next to nothing. There the movie ends.

I turned off the VCR profoundly depressed. I said to my wife, "That's the way many people see the world. Evil triumphs — The End." If I ever preach on Ahab stealing Nabal's vineyard, though, that movie will be a part of my introduction.

The questions I ask about ads are, *What do they want people to do? And how are they motivating them?* Marketers spend millions of research dollars to learn what motivates people. Watching their ads, we see the results of their research.

In one recent ad, a school appealed for new students, stating repeatedly that their graduates make more money. The school didn't promise its classes would make students deeper, better people, or open the door to a more fulfilling career. The carrot being dangled was money. In preaching, I can use that ad to raise the question of whether money alone is ultimately going to satisfy.

As another tributary for high-water preaching, I make it a point to converse with people different from me.

I've learned to make the most of the power of questions: How do you make your living? In your field of work, what are your biggest problems? Who are the successful people in your world? What makes people winners or losers to you? What do you have to worry about? If you could have anything in the world, what would it be?

I once met a man who owned a plastics manufacturing company. "How do you compete with the big boys in your trade?" I asked.

"Service," he responded. "I give my customers the best service." He went on to describe the lengths he went to give his customers what they want. I realized that today, the product may not be as important to people as the attitude and service that come along with it. That may make it into a sermon on evangelism sometime.

One of the most meaningful conversations I've had recently was with a person who has AIDS. He had been involved in a homosexual relationship with a man with whom he thought he had a "love-bonding relationship."

"He didn't tell me he had AIDS," he said sadly.

He described his fears of dying in a few years and his anger that someone he loved had done something that would kill him. He talked about his feelings of regret, of being ostracized, of wanting others to care but not sensing their care, of being sexually frustrated yet at the same time hating sex for its drawing power.

"I couldn't do to another human being what that man did to

me," he said.

Through all of this, he had become a Christian. Talking with him helped me better understand people in such situations. Such conversations feed my soul and add richness to preaching.

Soul Attention

The more full our souls, the more we can preach without running dry.

Of the many spiritual disciplines that enlarge spirit, mind, and soul, we need to find the ones that benefit us the most. I have a friend whose son has joined a monastery in pursuit of spirituality. He finds great benefit from the vow of silence and from long periods of meditation upon Scripture. Such disciplines have less benefit for me. But it is impossible for me to overstate how much my friendships with certain people have challenged me. Although being with large groups does more to drain me than stimulate me, I will rearrange my calendar just to spend a day or two with a friend.

We also need to recognize the difference between authentic growth and borrowed growth. I know a woman who has a tremendous appreciation for classical music. When she listens to a masterpiece, it is food for her soul. I envy her. I wish music stirred me as it does her. Sometimes when I hear her talk about music, I'm tempted to talk about music as she talks about music. But I would be impersonating a connoisseur.

In our early days as Christians and as preachers, we need mentors and models to get us started. The growth they inspire in us is authentic if their values truly become ours, not just something we value because so-and-so stresses it. But if we try to preach exactly as they do, the same life themes they had, we will lack integrity. If you keep doing it, eventually you're a counterfeit.

There's a difference between someone who derives great pleasure from meditating on a sunset and someone who meditates on sunsets because that's what "deep" people do. We can read in *Preachers and Preaching* what Martin Lloyd Jones says about the importance of urgency in preaching, but if we try to be more urgent without having the values and passions that produce urgency, our preaching will strike listeners as affected.

The ideas, themes, experiences, virtues, authors, and art that have gripped our souls are the ones that fill our preaching cup.

The number of issues that need to be addressed is so vast, the quantity of preaching material in Scripture so great, the needs of people so inexhaustible, a preacher couldn't finish the job in ten lifetimes. If we organize our sermonic work and stay full of God, more often than not, as we sit down to work out our sermons, we'll not only have something to say, we'll have more to say than time allows.

We can muster heroic acts of sacrifice, commitment, and self-denial for a while, but eventually if we don't pay attention to our personal needs, we run out of steam.

— Steve Brown

CHAPTER ELEVEN
Strength for the Weekly Grind

Ben Haden, pastor of First Presbyterian Church in Chattanooga, Tennessee, and an old friend, had spoken at a meeting in Miami, and I was driving him to the airport. At the time, in addition to pastoring, I was commuting by plane each week to Reformed Theological Seminary, where I served as adjunct preaching professor, and hosted an all-night radio program on Sunday nights (and sleeping most of Monday, my day off).

I felt I was handling it pretty well. Although I often tossed and turned at night, I would think, *I'll sleep better tomorrow night.*

Although at times I dealt with a load of unjustified anger or low-grade depression, I would brush it off as my having a bad week. People in church would say, "Pastor, you look tired," but that made me feel good. Besides, I felt, you can't pay much attention to that or you'll begin babying yourself. Anyway, I did take a day here or there golfing or at the beach.

On the way to the airport, Ben said, "Steve, you're close to a nervous breakdown."

That gave me pause; I didn't want to admit it, but after a little reflection, I realized he was right. I was exhausted.

Sometimes, when ministry pressure gets to me, I have a fantasy I go back to North Carolina and a simpler way of life. I become a disk jockey again (or better yet, a vinyl repairman), work nine to five, watch television, love people, and spend time with my family. There was a time when I said in jest — but was more serious than anyone knew — that if they'd let me bring my wife, I'd become a Trappist monk.

Many things can turn ministry into a weekly grind. Boredom. Too little time, too much to do. Limitless small problems that inflict death by a thousand cuts. Occasional crises that overwhelm.

Where can we find strength to plug away at ministry week-in, week-out? In particular, how can we find energy and creativity to preach effectively for decades on end?

Waking Sleeping Dogs

During the Revolutionary War, George Washington one day visited a church. Recognizing him, the pastor took off his hat. Washington said, "Reverend, put your hat back on. We both have done the same thing — what we were supposed to do."

Ministry is a weekly grind, but it's what we're supposed to do. Sometimes we may fantasize about different work or a different life, but if we're realistic, balanced persons, most weeks we simply go back and do what we have to do.

Nevertheless, though we muster heroic acts of sacrifice, commitment, and self-denial for a while, if we don't pay attention to our personal needs, we will eventually run out of steam. That affects all of ministry and especially our preaching.

In particular, I've discovered that sometimes we run through ministry like crazed zombies, refusing to back off, because we're not able to come to terms with some inner turmoil.

I share an office with the man who teaches psychology at Reformed Seminary. He has a cartoon on the wall that pictures a large auditorium with only three people seated in it, and the caption reads, "The Annual Convention of the Adult Children of Normal Parents."

Like most people, pastors carry issues from the past that affect their emotions and how they handle the weekly pressures of being pastors. Though we can deny them for a while, at some point we're going to have to deal with them.

I knew of my "sleeping dogs," but I didn't want to wake them: my father was an alcoholic, and I grew up hearing my mother threatening to leave him. When I was twelve, I confronted my father's mistress. You can imagine the loneliness, shame, anger, and fear in which I was raised.

Decades later, as a pastor, I functioned pretty well. I made it from morning to night. But eventually, I had so increased my workload (probably because I didn't want to face my inner turmoil), that I ran myself down. That's when my defenses started coming down; my childhood anger and fear surfaced, and I didn't know how to handle those volatile emotions.

A friend of mine had gone through a similar experience and talked to me about it. One day I said, "Lea, I'm going to wake these sleeping dogs, but I'll do it with a gun in my hand. If they bite me, I'm going to shoot them."

A short time later, Lea attended a meeting where I was speaking, and afterward he said to me, "I have a message from the Lord. Wake the dogs, but forget the gun. They don't have any teeth."

Over time I dealt with those issues, forgave my father, and released the sense of shame I had long experienced — it's a long story. But once I came to grips with my past hurts, I regained my equilibrium to perform active ministry for the long haul.

Riding the Wings of a Dove

I've preached when I didn't have a vibrant spiritual life, and I've preached when I was experiencing God's rich presence. The former is like peddling a one-speed bike up a long, steep hill; the latter, like riding the wings of a dove.

I became a Christian primarily for intellectual reasons and preached intellectually for years. Now and then I got "warm fuzzies," listening to a Christian musician, for instance, but that was as far as it went.

Thirteen years ago, I reached a crisis in my ministry. I was intellectually and homiletically prepared each week, but I was spiritually bereft. I was a Christian; I believed the doctrines — I wouldn't have endured what I was enduring in ministry otherwise! My preaching was reasonably effective. But I came to the point where my sin was more real to me than God. Everything was more real to me than God.

"God, I want to know you," I prayed. "I don't want to know you by hearsay. Whatever it takes, I want to know you."

That was the beginning of a long trek.

Independently of each other, three friends sent me *The Celebration of Discipline* by Richard Foster. That opened a door. I began reading the contemplatives, whom I had hardly known existed: St. John of the Cross, Theresa of Avila, Thomas Merton. I experimented with some of the spiritual disciplines, spending time in silence before God, for instance.

Over time, God came, sometimes as quiet peace, sometimes as overwhelming joy. It was a life-changing experience for me.

That prayer — "God, I want to know you; whatever it takes, I want to know you" — is the sort of desperate prayer we need to pray periodically in our lives.

And then once our souls have been restored, we have to figure out ways to maintain the intimacy. I think the key to that is not great faith or great discipline or great resolve but simple honesty.

In the movie *Fiddler on the Roof*, Tevya is a common man with an uncommon prayer life. The movie doesn't portray him as having great faith, but he prays honestly. He tells God how he feels. He's real. He doesn't try to impress God.

I need to be real with God. My morning devotional time is the one place where I'm not on stage, where I'm completely accepted. There I pour out my soul, telling God when I'm angry, when I'm joyful, weeping sometimes, singing at others.

Shortcuts

Time and energy are limited. Under the press of weekly responsibilities and emergencies at church, only so many sermons can receive our maximum effort. One way, then, to keep up strength for preaching is to learn a few shortcuts.

● *Repeat.* Our mothers told us if we didn't wait an hour after eating to go swimming, we would get cramps, drown, and die. That's a myth. Seminary professors tell students a similar myth: pastors should never repeat their sermons. They forget that during the Great Awakening, George Whitefield preached the same few sermons dozens, if not hundreds of times.

There are several good reasons to repeat sermon material:

First, if we repeat the average sermon one year later, nobody will likely notice except your spouse! People simply don't remember.

Second, a congregation turns over every few years. In Key Biscayne, at first I felt terrible about the 80 percent turnover we had every five years. Then I realized that took some of the pressure off to keep coming up with new material three or more times a week. Of the 20 percent who remained, half probably missed church the first time I preached the message.

Third, a lot of material is too good to be used only once. If an illustration blessed the majority of the congregation, I want to use it again at a later date. Some humorous stories make you laugh even the second and third time.

Naturally, you can overdo it. A friend of mine told how he had used the old footsteps illustration (where the sufferer's befuddlement at seeing only one set of footsteps in the sand is cleared up with the Lord's telling him he had been carried during those critical times) a third time within a year. After the third use, a person said,

"Thank you for that illustration, but I think three times is the limit."

As we repeat sermons, of course, we shouldn't slavishly repeat the entire sermon. We can add or subtract illustrations and points to keep it current. That alone can give the sermon a new feel.

I encourage pastors to develop "tracks," whole units of material we can use in a variety of settings. For instance, I have a series of talks that address the twelve prisons we find ourselves in: the prison of responsibility, the prison of guilt, the prison of legalism, and so on. I can take units of that material and plug them like a cassette tape into various messages and settings — a Bible study at someone's home, a youth retreat, in the newsletter. If used in a Sunday evening sermon, a track can be used several months later in a different Sunday morning sermon.

• *Wing it.* After you've attended Bible college and/or seminary and pastored for several years, you know more about the Christian life than 99 percent of your congregation. Especially in today's culture, we're not talking to biblically or homiletically sophisticated people. So, after a decade or two in ministry, I think we're justified now and then to "wing it."

Winging it doesn't mean not preparing at all, just trusting experience and the Holy Spirit to see you through some standard presentations (like what it means to be a member of a church, or how to become a Christian).

I teach communication seminars with R. C. Sproul. He tells preachers they shouldn't even take notes to the pulpit. Trust what you know and talk to people. Risk it, and go into the pulpit without anything. Sproul is the last person to advocate poor preparation. His message is that we can rely more on the deep well of past experience and study than we may be accustomed to.

During particularly busy weeks, I would risk like that on Wednesday night services. I would study the text and reflect on the presentation, but I wouldn't bother coming up with an extended outline. I'd prepare a sketchy outline and speak from it. What I lost in succinctness and clarity I gained in intimacy and impact.

Naturally, for tightly scheduled Sunday mornings, where clarity and conciseness are demanded, so is more preparation.

• *Borrow.* A California pastor wrote me a humorous letter: "I have a confession. Everybody in my congregation was criticizing my sermons, so I stole one of yours. You used an illustration about your cat, and I don't have a cat, so I changed that. Otherwise I preached your entire message.

"But I've never received so much criticism for a sermon!"

Borrowing may not solve all our problems, then, but it will help out with at least one: the need to find fresh illustrative material.

So I feel free to ransack others' sermons for illustrations, ideas, and outlines. People say to me, "I use a lot of your stories." I respond, "That's okay, I stole them from someone else!" In the end, I believe we're all on the same team. Naturally, I try to give due credit if the story is unusual or well-developed.

I draw the line, though, on borrowing entire sermons. Phillips Brooks's famous definition of preaching — truth through personality — is true. A borrowed sermon will sound foreign on my tongue. It just won't impact the congregation.

Weekly Habits

We've all heard statements like "You ought to be on your knees more than you're at your typewriter." After my spiritual breakthrough, my heart is naturally drawn in that direction, but I also know one key to having strength for weekly preaching is developing some weekly habits that keep me fresh.

The problem is that a lot of the advice I've heard over the years just doesn't work for me. Here, then, are a few principles, somewhat contrarian, that I work by.

• *Don't get organized — unless you have to.* I'm not naturally organized. If I try to get organized because I read a time management book or because I ought to or because someone says I should — rather than because I have to — those new systems are doomed to failure. There's no motivation to keep them up. But if it's do or die, the need to stay organized continues to compel me.

I never organized my library until I had to. I always knew where my favorite books were. But then I got to the point where I couldn't find the quotes anymore, and so the library finally got organized, saving hours of preparation time.

If your life is copacetic, enjoy what God has given you. As pressures increase, read a time-management book. Never do today what you can put off till tomorrow.

• *Wait until the last minute.* I've discovered that I work better under the gun. I cannot get motivated to work on a sermon, for instance, until the preaching opportunity is around the corner. So there's no point in beating myself to prepare way ahead of time; I just won't do it.

At Key Biscayne, I wrote my Sunday sermon on Saturday, starting at four in the morning and going however long it took, sometimes writing until late into the night, sometimes needing only an hour or two, but generally it took eight to fifteen hours of nose to the grindstone. I wrote Sunday night's sermon on Sunday afternoon. Generally I spent most of Wednesday writing my sermon for that night.

• *Don't read what you should.* Don't read a book merely because it's good for you, because a high-profile leader recommended it, because you have to. Don't read a tome on theology merely because your seminary professor said pastors should read one theology book a year. Life is too short. Eat your dessert first. Read what you enjoy, what interests and stimulates you, what opens the windows and lets in a fresh breeze.

Most of my reading doesn't end up in my sermons, but it's provocative or fulfilling. I read or scan three to four books a week, but frankly there aren't a lot of religious books now that I read from cover to cover. I never read theology books anymore. The magazines I read regularly are *Time, National Review, Reader's Digest*, and *Christianity Today*.

• *Appear superficial.* I can't tell you how many times I've been devastated by criticism from someone I respect saying, "All he does is tell stories." Now I take it as a compliment.

Perhaps there was a time when preachers could get by without illustrations, when people would sit and listen to straight exposition of a text, but that day is past. In our media-dominated culture, people think visually. If you can't illustrate, you aren't going to communicate (if something can't be illustrated, it's irrelevant anyway). Many look down their noses at story telling, but they do so at great peril to their ministry.

So as much as I like to study theology and philosophy, my main homiletic antennae are usually up for good illustrations. When I find one, I either photocopy or write it down, but I don't file it alphabetically. I have a folder in which I collect illustrations as they come, and I regularly leaf through it, rereading what's there. A good illustration can be used ten different ways, so most of the material I collect finds its way into a message within a few months.

Illustration books are my safety net. You've heard professors say you should never use illustration books. Well, they're lying through their teeth. They're using the same teaching notes they've been using for twenty years; pastors are out there scrambling for three messages a week. Use everything you can get your hands on, anything that works. If you only get two good illustrations out of a book, it's worth the price (and you'll find more than two).

Tell the congregation you'd sell your soul for a good illustration, and ask them to give you ones that catch their attention. When you use an illustration from someone in the congregation, mention the contributor's name from the pulpit. Soon you'll have dozens of research assistants.

• *Stop being nice.* If you're going to find sufficient time to put into sermon preparation, you're going to have to develop a "mean streak." In a church, something's always broken. If you're at the beck and call of small people who want you to do small things, you'll never get enough study time. You'll spend all of your time pleasing people.

Once I put in the Sunday bulletin the hours I would be available for counseling and conversation. Some people were angry about that, feeling that their pastor ought to be available to them twenty-four hours a day.

So I responded to those who complained: "I will be available twenty-four hours a day for emergencies, and especially for a funeral — yours." It was a half-joke, and people knew it.

If you can learn to say no (even though you feel guilty about it), you'll communicate you're not everyone's mother. That will help lay people take increasing responsibility for one another. Then you can have sufficient time for study *and* be available for moments of real need.

I knew Ben Haden as a man with incredible insight into people, so I took his comment about my potential breakdown seriously. Within a few weeks, I pulled out of the radio program and began taking more time off. The more sane my schedule became, the more I realized how right Ben was. I had been on the edge, but while it was happening, I couldn't read it.

My life verse is "Whatever your hand finds to do, do it with all your might." Since I'm poor at recognizing when I'm getting too weary, I need to listen to the warnings of people who know me.

I also need to pay attention to my emotional and spiritual life, and to my weekly habits. When I do, my life is renewed by the Holy Spirit, and that means my preaching will continue to renew others, week by week, year by year.

One reason the modern world ignores our preaching is because it rarely hears anything from us it cannot hear from Dear Abby or Leo Buscaglia.
— *William Willimon*

Preaching to the Disinclined

A Christian fraternity and sorority group wanted me to talk on being a Christian on Duke's campus.

"For starters," I said, "I expect that by this weekend some of you will be in bed with somebody you're not married to, maybe with somebody in this group. What could I say to you tonight to give you the resources to refuse to do that?"

They got mad. Some of them said, "Wait. We're a *Christian* group. How dare you say something like that!"

"You look normal to me," I replied, "and I know the statistics, that few college students remain virgins any longer. I'm not doing this to attack you; I'm a preacher, and I'm supposed to be giving you what you need to live a Christian life."

After the group calmed down, one student said, "But why do preachers always act like sex is the biggest sin in the world?"

"That's a good question," I said. "Sounds like you know your Bible, because sex isn't the biggest problem according to the Bible. Still, we assume that if we can just get you to say no to this, a relatively little thing, there's no telling where we could go from here."

We live and minister in a culture that scoffs, gets riled, or worse, patronizes with polite interest the truths we preach. An important role of today's pastor is preaching truth to a disinclined world, to unbelievers who don't take us seriously, to nominal Christians who don't want to "overdo religion." How do we convince such people that there is something better, deeper, more significant they can give their lives to?

It's in the Fine Print

Let me begin with a caution: let's not start feeling sorry for ourselves, as if our current, increasingly pagan situation is all that new.

It would be fun, I think, to ask the writer of Acts, "What do you think about the modern disinterest in the gospel?"

Luke probably would say, "Has anybody physically beat you for preaching the gospel? That's the response we got."

Luke, of course, has amazing confidence in the power of the Word, despite the hardships; his story is one of the Word leaping over boundaries. Some, in fact, have accused Luke of homiletical triumphalism: "Preaching makes things happen! Look at Peter — he preached, and a couple thousand people showed up for baptism."

But triumphalism? Stephen preaches a few verses later, and they beat the stuffing out of him. Christian communicators can hope for baptisms, but we have to recognize the "beatings" that also may come our way. Our modern dilemma is not new: preachers throughout Christian history have struggled with delivering the

Good News to an indifferent and sometimes hostile world. It's always been listed in the fine print of the Christian preacher's job description.

It's been a long time, though, since I've had the tar beaten out of me for the gospel (or since I've had two thousand seek baptism!). More typically I've gotten the Gentile response in Acts: scoffing or patronizing disinterest. It's like Agrippa or Felix, who say things like, "My, we haven't heard anything this interesting in a long time. We ought to get together and talk about this again. Of course, everything is relative, and we don't believe one way or the other . . ."

I think Luke might say to us, "What you're reading as modern disinterest is just the good old pagan response to the gospel. Resistance is nothing new."

The response we get, however, isn't the issue. The issue is to bear apostolic witness, regardless of how hard it is.

My friend Stanley Hauerwas and I were speaking at a gathering of Methodist ministers. During the following question-and-answer time, one of them stood up and said, "I preached on racial justice in my church, and things went from bad to worse. My children were mocked at school. And the congregation called the bishop and complained about my sermons. Then my wife was fired from her job. As a result we had to move; I was assigned to a church in another city."

My heart went out to this poor brother. But Hauerwas's heart didn't. "God is a nasty employer," said Hauerwas, with a shrug of his shoulders. "He's a big God, not a fake. And that's what it's like to work for a real God. Does anybody else have anything to say?" No one whined after that.

When we signed on to work for God, we signed on for the baptisms as well as the beatings. We should expect nothing less than the reaction the apostles got: opposition or just plain befuddlement.

From the Bottom Up

Let's admit it: one reason the modern world ignores our preaching is because it rarely hears anything from us it cannot hear from Dear Abby or Leo Buscaglia. I've met people who've given up on us because we're so bland. I rarely hear that people leave our churches because we're too involved in social activism, too liberal, or too conservative. I do, though, hear a lot of people confess, "I'm bored. I never hear anything interesting. The sermon is so drearily predictable."

Many are indifferent to our message because we've often softened it, tried to make it palatable to modern ears. People don't want that; instead, living as they do in a relativistic, lost culture, they desperately yearn for a moral compass.

One day I was in a sociology class to talk on marriage. Divorce came up, and I was saying, "Well, here are the words of Jesus, and there's been a debate within the church over their interpretation." I was trying to leave room for the many nuances.

Suddenly a student broke in and said, "This is just the kind of mealy-mouthed crap the clergy is saying these days: 'Divorce is not right, but on the other hand it may be okay.' "

Other students pitched in, "Yeah, yeah. You tell him!"

After class I pulled the student aside and asked about his response. I was surprised when he said, "Well, my old man left us for his secretary when I was 16." We spent the next two hours talking about that.

The cultural flotsam of the sixties looks different when you're looking at it from the bottom up. Divorce isn't seen as "an exciting new option for personal freedom" but as abandonment by one of the parents.

For many people, the teachings of the Bible are radically novel ideas. I was talking to a young woman on Duke's campus who'd been working with Habitat for Humanity in Americus, Georgia. She mentioned her astonishment at their discipline: "One thing about that group — you can't have sex down there with other people."

"Oh, really?"

"Yeah, they kick people out for that. They said they've found that sex among group members destroys community. They have too many important things that need to be done for people to be messing up everything by sleeping together."

It was a new insight for her. She was intrigued that people thought something more important than sex.

Even many who've grown up in church have been utterly unscathed by Christian morality.

I once asked a Duke student if he intends to have sex before marriage, and he said, "Yeah. Why not?"

"You grew up in a church, and you don't think anything is wrong with that?" I asked.

"I never heard that anything was wrong with it," he said. "What do you mean?" He was utterly naive, though he had grown up in a Christian church.

People are ripe for a voice that gives them something worth living and dying for.

Engaging Truths

At the same time, we mustn't ever kid ourselves about people's motives for showing up in worship.

I asked one student who'd been ushering several Sundays, "How do you like chapel?"

"I like it," he said.

"What do you think about the preaching?"

"Well, I like that, too."

"What do you like about it?"

"I just, ah, like it."

I kept pressing him for specifics. Finally he said, "Look, Dr. Willimon, I'll be honest with you. I come to chapel to meet women."

"Thank you," I said. "This has done me good. In case I should ever become presumptuous, I will remember this conversation."

I've had to come to terms with the fact that people come to church for a host of reasons — most of them bad, theologically. Though ultimately they are searching for meaning in their lives, we shouldn't naively assume people are hanging on our every word. If we're going to try to reach the disinclined, we're going to have to preach in a way that engages their attention.

In the book Stanley Hauerwas and I wrote together, *Preaching to Strangers*, Hauerwas remarks that one of my sermons was marvelously entertaining. I took that as a great compliment; boredom is not a virtue. I don't mind entertaining, as long as I'm faithful to the text.

When I was in high school, my sister gave me a book entitled, *Public Speaking as Your Listeners Like It*, which impacts my preaching to this day. Its main point was the ho-hum rule: assume your listeners are never interested in what you're interested in. The book recommended picturing the listener as a guy who's been dragged there by his wife and doesn't like the looks of you. He thinks he knows more than you do and is incessantly looking at his watch.

Your job: to convince him your subject is the most important thing he will hear the rest of his life.

The ho-hum rule doesn't mean I eschew less palatable subjects. Just because my listeners could care less about the Jebusites doesn't mean I don't preach on the Jebusites. My task as a preacher is to convince them that they really do care about the Jebusites. To do this requires us to use an array of communication techniques to get them to care.

One way I do this is by being controversial. I intentionally assault the congregation with the gospel so they'll huddle together for protection.

One Sunday before Christmas, a guest preacher didn't show up because of icy weather, so I preached a spur-of-the-moment sermon on John the Baptist. In the sermon I said, "Imagine putting John the Baptist on a Christmas card and saying, 'Our thoughts for you at this special time of year are best expressed by the one who said, "You brood of vipers! Who told you to flee from the wrath to come?" Merry Christmas.' "

People kept telling me afterward what a great sermon I'd preached. I thought the sermon was a little harsh as I looked back at it. So I spent the rest of that week asking people, "Why was that a good sermon?"

They said, "You were right, and we're ready for some honesty about our condition."

Another way to engage people is to speak frankly and strongly about issues people face.

In one sermon on discipleship, I said, "Look, our capitalistic economy would love to keep you having sex all the time. They'd love to sell you blue jeans and perfume; this is the way they anesthetize you. They want to convince you there's nothing more significant in life than orgasm.

"They want to convince you this is what adults do, that this is the most important part of your humanity. It makes a whole lot of difference in the way you look, how you dress, and the kind of glances you give. They want you to believe that. And you have been converted into that beautifully.

"But it's a lie," I said. "I hate to break the news to you: sex is not all that great. It's all right. I know what you're thinking: you think I'm saying this because I'm forty. But I've been doing it a lot longer than any of you have — and I say it's not that big a deal. You're about as good at it now as you'll ever get. And you can't get saved doing it."

"Isn't it funny how the Bible hardly ever mentions sex?" I concluded. "Jesus didn't want to talk about sex; he wanted to talk about discipleship. Jesus is only interested in sex as it relates to discipleship. If it keeps you from being a faithful disciple, it's a big deal. Otherwise, have a good time."

A student once said to me, "This morning's message was a typical Willimon sermon. You went in, you hit them in the gut, and you left." I have a dual purpose in being controversial and frank: the message of the Bible is controversial and frank, and such preaching engages people.

The Serious Role of Humor

Another way I engage the listener is through humor. Listeners are vulnerable to humor. One of my more delightful vocations in life is demonstrating how wonderfully funny and ironic the gospel is.

Jesus tells an ironic parable in which he compares a banquet to the kingdom of God. In Luke's account, a man throws a party and sends invitations to those lucky enough to receive them. Nobody shows up, however. The man gets ticked off and then invites the local riffraff, who have no where to go on a Saturday night.

Then he essentially says, "Oh heck, we've cooked all this food. Go on out and bring in anybody. Bring in the good and the bad. You brought in these nice crippled people. Go bring in anybody."

Jesus' point: the kingdom of God is a party we wouldn't be caught dead attending. It's a ridiculous, humorous parable that sets up the listener for its punch line: we spend our whole lives avoiding certain people only to wake up and find that, in the kingdom, they're the people we have to eat next to for eternity. I find that story wonderfully entertaining and funny but also biting. Its humor sets up the listener for the hard truth.

Martin Luther King once preached a sermon in which he recalled being stabbed by a deranged woman. He mentioned that, after the stabbing, the newspapers reported that a doctor had said, "If Dr. King had sneezed he would have died." A little white girl from Connecticut, he says, later wrote him a letter saying, "Dear Dr. King, I'm real glad you didn't sneeze."

So King says, "If I'd sneezed, I wouldn't have been down in Birmingham." Then, "Well, if I had sneezed, I wouldn't have been able to go to Stockholm to get the Nobel Prize." He goes on and on, listing the places he wouldn't have been if he had sneezed. His wry humor invigorated the sermon, so that the congregation responded, shouting *Amens* and laughing with him.

Vitality Set Loose

Ultimately the only thing keeping me at delivering God's outrageous truths to the disinclined is that I'm convinced this Christian stuff is true. What ought to cause me to lie awake at night is not that somebody found me boring or my message outdated but whether I've been faithful to my appointed calling to preach the Word.

And one reason I continue to think this stuff is true is what happens as a result of preaching it. At Duke, it's like I'm in a laboratory, and all the ministerial variables are stripped away until only preaching is being tested. I've seen time and again that preaching can take the unbeliever into belief, and the nonchalant believer into deeper commitment.

Several years ago Jim Wallis, editor of *Sojourners* magazine, preached at Duke Chapel. He gave his radical *Sojourners* pitch, and two days later a Duke freshman told me, "Dr. Willimon, I want to thank you for bringing that man down here. I went back to my dorm, and I called my parents and told them I wanted my name removed from the rolls of the church I grew up in."

"Oh, no!" I said. "Why would you do something like that? I don't want angry calls from your mother."

"I grew up in that church — a Christian all that time," he replied, "and nobody ever spoke about Jesus and the poor. I did what Wallis said: I looked through my Bible, and it's unbelievable how much it says about the poor and the rich, and about God's love."

This kid was bubbling about how he was going to spend his Christmas break working for Habitat for Humanity.

It's beautiful to see that kind of vitality let loose.

Sometimes even the disinclined are radically transformed by the power of the gospel's truth. Scary, isn't it?

Preaching fools you. It looks like a matter of exegesis and oratory. It turns out to be blood, sweat, toil, and tears.
— Mark Galli

Epilogue

One pastor wrote to one of our contributors, lamenting his ministry: "I've been a pastor seven years now. It has been very hard. I came out of seminary very idealistic. The reality of parish ministry was shattering. . . . I really believed that when a congregation was loved and presented with a clear presentation of the gospel, they would fall into line. They would be saved. They would go forth. How naive."

What pastor does not know this discouragement? Sometimes we feel as if we preach in hot, flat stretches; all we see for miles are heat waves floating lazily from the white sand, and perhaps some cacti and a lizard or two. We feel lonely — a voice crying in the wilderness doesn't even echo back to us. And we feel foolish. *How naive!*

We are right to be disheartened. Preaching has always been, and always will be, an eternally significant but eternally trying task. As our authors have noted, the pulpit will always be one of ministry's most intense pressure points. Preaching fools you. It looks like a matter of exegesis and oratory. It turns out to be blood, sweat, toil, and tears.

But we are wrong to think ourselves naive. Once in awhile we simply need to be reminded, as we are in this book, that there is no other way by which people can be saved in Christ except through loving, clear preaching — "How can they believe in the one of whom they have not heard? And how can they hear without someone preaching to them?"

Yes, it is as simple and naive as that.

And we believe it. No, we *know* it, somewhere deep, deep within. That's precisely why, as we trudge through the desert of despair, we continue to proclaim to the cacti and lizards. That's why, after we've mentally loaded the U-Haul, we mentally reshelve our commentaries. That's why, after we've gone on a preaching strike (for six days), we preach again. And again. And again.

We are like Jeremiah: "But if I say, 'I will not mention his name, his word is in my heart like a fire, a fire shut up in my bones. I am weary of holding it in; indeed, I cannot."

In the end, the heat within is greater than the heat without. And so we preach, in the relative cool of the desert.